LIFE IN FOREST
AND JUNGLE

Illustrated by Nancy Lou Gahan

LIFE
IN FOREST
AND
JUNGLE

Richard Perry

VOLUME IV: THE MANY WORLDS OF WILDLIFE SERIES

Taplinger Publishing Company   *New York*

First Edition
Published in the United States in 1976 by
TAPLINGER PUBLISHING CO., INC.
New York, New York

Published simultaneously in the Dominion of Canada by Burns & MacEachern, Toronto

Library of Congress Catalog Card Number: 74-21573

ISBN 0-8008-4799-7

Designed by Mollie M. Torras

Grateful acknowledgement is made for permission to quote from the following copyright material:

The Amazon: A Photographic Survey by E. Schulthess. Translated by H. A. Frey and C. Wayland. Copyright © 1962 by Emil Schulthess. The extract by Emil Egli is reprinted with the permission of William Collins Sons & Co. Ltd.

Budongo: A Forest and Its Chimpanzees by Vernon Reynolds. Copyright © 1965 by Vernon Reynolds. Reprinted with the permission of Methuen & Co. Ltd. and Doubleday & Company, Inc.

Catch Me a Colobus by Gerald Durrell. Copyright © 1972 by Gerald Durrell. Reprinted with the permission of William Collins Sons & Co. Ltd. and the Viking Press.

The Company of Animals by Ronald McKie. Copyright © 1965 by Ronald McKie. Reprinted with the permission of Angus & Robertson Publishers Ltd. and Sanford J. Greenburger Associates, Inc.

In the Shadow of Man by Jane van Lawick-Goodall. Copyright © 1971 by Hugo and Jane van Lawick-Goodall. Reprinted by permission of William Collins Sons & Co. Ltd. and Houghton Mifflin Company.

Mato Grosso: Last Virgin Land by Anthony Smith. Copyright © 1971 by The Royal Society and The Royal Geographical Society. Reprinted with the permission of Michael Joseph Limited and E. P. Dutton & Co., Inc.

The Natural History of the Elephant by Sylvia Sikes. Copyright © 1971 by Sylvia Sikes. Reprinted with the permission of Weidenfeld (Publishers) Limited and American Elsevier Publishing Co., Inc.

Orang-Utan by Barbara Harrisson. Copyright © 1972 by Barbara Harrisson. Reprinted with the permission of William Collins Sons & Co. Ltd. and Doubleday & Company, Inc.

To the memory of
Dick Taplinger

ACKNOWLEDGEMENTS

Once again to the Morpeth Reference Department of the Northumberland County Library for supplying me with several scores of essential books and papers, and also to the following authors and publishers for permission to quote from their books: *Forest, Steppe and Tundra* by Maud D. Haviland (Cambridge University Press, 1926); *My Year with the Woodpeckers* by Heinz Sielmann (Barrie & Rockcliffe, 1959); *Mammals of North America* by Victor H. Cahalane (Macmillan, New York, 1947, 1966); *The Land and Wildlife of Africa* by Archie Carr and the Editors of Time-Life Books (1964); Emil Egli, in *The Amazon: A Photographic Survey* by E. Schulthess (Collins, 1962, and Simon & Schuster, 1963); *Mato Grosso: Last Virgin Land* by Anthony Smith (Michael Joseph and E. P. Dutton, 1971); *Tropical Wild Life in British Guiana* by William Beebe (New York Zoological Society, 1917); *Wildlife of Mexico* by A. Starker Leopold (University of California Press, 1959); *In the Amazon Jungle* by Algot Lange (G. P. Putnam, 1912); *The Perpetual Forest* by W. B. Collins (Staples Press, 1958); *An Introduction to the Behaviour of Ants* by John Sudd (Edward Arnold and St. Martin's Press, 1967); *Catch Me a Colobus* by Gerald Durrell (Collins and Viking Press, 1972); *Big Game and Pygmies* by Cuthbert Christy (Macmillan, London,

9

1924); *The Natural History of the African Elephant* by Sylvia Sikes (Weidenfeld & Nicolson and American Elsevier, 1971); *Budongo* by Vernon Reynolds (Methuen and Doubleday, 1965); *Carl Akeley's Africa* by Mary L. J. Akeley (Gollancz and Dodd, Mead, 1931); *In the Shadow of Man* by Jane van Lawick-Goodall (Collins and Houghton Mifflin, 1971); *The Year of the Gorilla* (University of Chicago Press, 1964, and Collins, 1965) and *The Deer and the Tiger* (University of Chicago Press, 1967) by George B. Schaller; *Orang-Utan* by Barbara Harrisson (Collins, 1962, and Doubleday, 1963); *The Company of Animals* by Ronald McKie (Angus & Robertson, 1965, and Harcourt, Brace & World, 1966); *The Twilight of India's Wildlife* by Balakrishna Seshadri (John Baker and Fernhill House, 1969); *The Malay Archipelago* by Alfred Russell Wallace (Macmillan, 1869, reprinted by Peter Smith); *Birds of Paradise and Bower Birds* by E. Thomas Gilliard (Weidenfeld & Nicolson and Natural History Press, 1969); *A Territory of Birds* by Michael Sharland (Angus & Robertson, 1964); and finally, to Van Nostrand-Reinhold, publishers of *Grzimek's Animal Encyclopedia* (no date), and to the Editor of *Animals* (now *Wildlife*) for "The Monkeys of Barro Colorado Island" by David Chivers, "Lyrebirds of Sherbrooke" by Graham Pizzey, and "Birds That Build Bowers" by John Warham.

CONTENTS

ILLUSTRATIONS

Introduction

It is a pleasant surprise to learn that more than a quarter of Earth's land surface still carries some 15 million square miles of forests, which can be broadly classified as northern coniferous, temperate deciduous and tropical rain-forest. But for how much longer? Already man is beginning an all-out assault on the Amazon's vast primeval jungle, and trans-continental highways are being gouged through its wilderness; and who knows how many thousands of square miles of the Siberian taiga are being leveled by the Russians? Yet one has only to read the most recent books and papers on the wildlife of the South American jungle or, for that matter, of India's, or of the African rain-forest, to be astonished at how little is known even at this late date about the habits of relatively common animals. Indeed, it is no exaggeration to say that we do not know very much more about those inhabiting the South American jungle and swamp-forest than we did last century in the days of such pioneer naturalists as Baron von Humboldt, Thomas Belt and H. S. Bates, who were prepared to spend years in the field under atrocious conditions; while if some of the birds and mammals and insects of the gentle woodlands of England and the wilder forests of North America are better known, their life-histories still pose many problems.

In writing this fourth volume in The Many Worlds of Wildlife series I have been made ever more aware of these gaps in our knowledge, and also of the indivisibility of Nature. Who would suppose that, for instance, there was any relationship between wood ants and bees, termites and parrots or kingfishers, partridges and wild boars, or vultures and palm trees?

RICHARD PERRY

Northumberland, 1975

1: Inhabitants of Taiga and Muskeg

The eighth wonder of the world, the coniferous forests of spruce, fir, larch, pine, hemlock and cedar girdle the northern hemisphere for 8,000 miles. Their seemingly endless continuity is, or was, broken only by the large rivers flowing to the Arctic Ocean, by mountain ranges such as the Urals and the Mackenzies, and by the Atlantic and Pacific oceans. Their empire extends from the arctic tundra to such southern bastions as northern Poland in Europe and the St. Lawrence in North America. Moreover, sheltered river valleys enable the conifers to advance into the tundra many miles north of the normal timber line: just as in similar conditions silver birches and aspens, and to a lesser degree willows and alders, are able to make extensive intrusions into the coniferous forests from their southern edge; but the oaks, those characteristic trees of Europe and the Far East, are totally absent.

Although the trees in a primeval forest may stand so close together that a man is hard put to it to squeeze between their trunks, which are in any case rendered further impassable by their tangle of dead branches, a characteristic feature of the coniferous forest as a whole is the swamp forest, known as muskeg in Canada and as taiga in Siberia. The latter is so inconceivably vast that its 4½ million square miles of forest and bog and water cover an area one-third greater than the USA, and form a mosaic of forest-tarns and lakes, hundreds of thousands of bogs whitened with cotton sedge, rolling heaths and moors, and immense stretches of pure sand covered with pine woods and birch groves. The taiga's ground vegetation of mosses, lichens and dwarf plants resembles that of the tundra, but is much denser and choked with rush and sedge and large clumps of knee-deep or head-high willow and other bushes.

No one has described the taiga more graphically than Maud D. Haviland did fifty years ago:

> Seen from one of the great rivers, the taiga is like the sea in its immensity and monotony. . . . The vastness . . . is realised most intensely at dawn. While the ground below is still in darkness, birds perch on the tops of the trees to await the approach of light. Suddenly an ousel, far away to the eastward, begins to pipe faintly; and as the minutes pass, another and another, nearer and nearer, join in the chorus, until every tree bursts into a paean of song, which in turn is taken up by the expectant multitude in the forests to the westward. It seems as if the great wooded shoulder of the earth, rolling eastwards into the sunrise, awakes one songster after another, until Asia and Europe, from Pacific to Atlantic, are linked together by a chain of thrushes' music.
>
> When the river bank is left behind . . . dark spreading branches shut out the light . . . twigs and boles are hoary with lichen. . . . In the deepest shade even mosses are starved out, and the earth is smothered with a . . . muffling blanket of pine-needles, the leaf-fall of years. Where a tree falls, there it lies; and as you walk, you are apt to slip down, through sodden debris, knee-deep into the heart of a stump. . . . The shade and the silence are both oppressive. The sudden call of a bird, such as the goblin cry of the cuckoo, *Cuculus optatus*, is startling. . . . After crossing a mile or two of this forest, stooping under branches, squeezing between sap-

lings, and stumbling over broken boughs and mouldering stumps, it is a relief to emerge even into one of the moss-bogs, where at least one can see the sun and feel the wind. . . .
All animal life is hidden, except when a colony of fieldfares is startled into harsh screams or a sandpiper flies away crying mournfully. . . . Except for a few rodents, such as voles and squirrels, the mammals are hidden in the depths of the forest in summer. . . . Even bird life . . . is readily overlooked. Drawn by the need for light, many species nest and feed at a considerable height from the ground; and . . . the naturalist knows them only as silhouettes against the sky. . . . Conspicuous colouring in nature depends much on the background . . . a scarlet grosbeak in the dark taiga is as arresting as a flash of red light. . . . Most exquisite of all are the mealy redpolls, which are pearl-grey and pink. In summer they haunt the tops of larch and birch trees, and their frosted rose-leaf plumage, against a lattice of blue sky and dark twigs, is one of the most beautiful sights in the forest.

The animals that live in these northern forests where the air is dry and skies predominantly clear, have to adapt themselves to a habitat that is frozen or snow-covered for the greater part of the year. However, when the snow melts during the brief hot summer, rivers often overflow and flood low-lying forest, while the muskegs rapidly thaw out to much greater depths than the floor of the forest which, growing in dense stands and almost shutting out the sunlight, remains cool. On the other hand the forest floor is protected during the long cold winters by the evergreen canopy of interwoven branches, and does not freeze as deeply as the open swamp. In the dense spruce forests indeed snow may exceptionally lie like a blanket on the canopy, preventing the floor from freezing at all.

The global uniformity of taiga and forest is naturally paralleled by a similar uniformity among its inhabitants. Moose—the elk of Europe, whereas in North America the elk is the wapiti, a red deer—the various members of the weasel family and brown bears, for example, occur anywhere from Scandinavia east— about to Labrador. The gigantic moose, which may stand 7½ feet at the shoulder and weigh 1,800 pounds, are everywhere in the coniferous forest, and are the most widely distributed fauna in the taiga. But although there are said to be hundreds of thousands of moose in Canada, it is Sweden that boasts the largest population, relative to its area, of any region, and despite an annaul hunting kill of between 20,000 and 30,000, the Swedish stock is actually increasing.

Though usually associated in America with the virgin spruce forest, the moose's true habitat is to be found in the groves of willow and aspen that surround the bogs, and particularly the secondary growth that springs up after the mature primeval forest has been felled or burned, for whereas the dense undergrowth in mature forest is low in proteins, that in secondary forest is rich in them. In 5 square miles of such country a moose may spend its whole life. Its long legs, raising it 4½ feet above the ground, and gargantuan stride enable it to move through the tangled underbrush with surprising agility in what Ivan T. Sanderson has described as "a sort of monstrous prance with a jog-trot gait so that its enormous hoofs come up level with its belly, alternately front right and back left and front left and back right." Long legs make it possible for a moose to wade belly-deep in lakes and beaver ponds, preferably not more than 6 feet deep, and with long neck submerged for sixty seconds or longer at a time, feed on its favorite water-lilies, almost denuding some lakes of these. By rearing on its hind legs it can browse young conifers to a height of 9 feet, and to 14 feet in the winter when elevated by hard-trodden ramps of snow. Moreover, by running its chin up and along branches, it can bend them down from a height of 20 feet and strip their leaves; or, by riding down sap-

Moose

lings or brittle 20-foot aspens between its forelegs, feed on their
tops, clamping on the leafy twigs with its pendulous lips. Moose
can thus tap feed beyond the reach of any other herbivore. In
the winter they feed on the buds and twigs of conifers and
willows and on the bark of aspens which, according to Victor
H. Cahalane, they gouge off with a slanting upward cut of their
lower incisors; but, since they lack front teeth and incisors in the
upper jaw and cannot therefore bite out chunks of bark, they
prefer to work on fallen trees. Long legs enable them to negoti-

ate snow 3 feet deep, but when storms pile up the snow they must herd up, though not normally gregarious, in "yards" of trampled snow where twigs and bark are available, and where they can scrape down to berries and such evergreen plants as Labrador tea and wintergreens.

Moose and other inhabitants of northern forests are equipped to lead an active life in temperatures as low as minus 50 degrees F. Large tufts of hair on the varying hare's feet serve for snowshoes, as does the thick winter growth of hair on the sides and soles of the lynx's enormous "powderpuff" feet, increasing their surface spread by 2 inches. The life-histories of hare as prey and lynx as predator are inextricably linked. Although hares are also preyed on by bobcats, foxes and wolves, hawks, eagles and great horned and snowy owls, the combined toll taken by all these predators cannot control their numbers, and every nine or ten years their populations reach a peak. When the snows come in a peak year the hares, having nibbled off all the ground vegetation during the autumn and early winter, then gnaw the bark off almost every reachable sapling, though especially those of pines, cedars, birches and poplars. Eventually they exhaust all sources of food, and mass starvation and disease result in a rapid decline in their numbers. This is paralleled the following year by a similar crash in the numbers of lynxes and, in lesser degree, those of the other predators; but lynxes are especially and curiously affected, for though in normal years they also prey on a variety of mammals from mice to young deer and such birds as grouse, ptarmigan and duck, there is evidence that after a crash in the hare population, they may ignore other forms of prey, although these are present.

That ferocious carnivore, the wolverine, is also equipped with broad paws and splayed toes for snow travel and is, reputedly, able to cover at a clumsy gallop 40 miles without rest in deep snow. In such conditions it runs down roe deer and musk deer, and even full-grown wapiti, caribou and reindeer or young moose, springing on to the back of its quarry when it flounders in the snow and perhaps riding it for several hundred yards before ultimately bringing it down by biting its neck and vertebrae. It is true that the wolverine is the largest member of the weasel family, but nevertheless it displays phenomenal strength and aggressiveness for an animal not much more than 3 feet long including its tail, standing only 15 to 18 inches at the shoulder, and weighing as little as 25 pounds and at most 70 pounds. It routs coyotes and bears from their prey, attacks lynxes, and has been known to kill pumas, while wolves go out of their way to avoid it. It probably finds it more difficult to obtain food during the four summer months than during the eight winter months, for it is not swift enough to run down deer when there is no snow, and must depend for food on green shoots and the eggs and young of ground-nesting birds, and later in the summer on berries, cedar nuts, wasps' nests, lemmings, carrion, an occasional wapiti or caribou calf, or a porcupine.

The coniferous forest is the true habitat of the North American porcupines which, unlike their relatives in the Old World, are tree climbers; but their numbers are decreasing with the clearing of the forests and also because of persecution by lumbermen, since they are destructive to trees. In winter, for example, a porcupine may occupy a conifer for a whole week, stuffing itself with bark and greenery until it has almost stripped the tree of its needles. Wolverines are, however, clumsy in grappling with porcupines, and many are killed by quills penetrating their throats or stomach walls; whereas their relatives, the fishers, have learned to kill them by flipping them over with a dexterous paw and attacking their soft underparts, though they too are sometimes severely injured by quills.

During the interglacial eras, when there was a widespread formation of moorlands, wolverines were able to colonize immense areas of what is today coniferous forest throughout the northern hemisphere and, like lynxes and brown bears, they are true forest animals; but just as persecution has driven lynxes and bears into mountainous regions or deep into the taiga, so in the USSR wolverines have been banished to treeless regions in the mountains and out on to the tundra. In this environment they are reputed not to kill their own prey, but to rely mainly on the carcases of animals killed but not eaten by wolves. In such circumstances several wolverines collect at a carcase and remain beside it for some days until it has been entirely consumed. But one assumes that only hunger could drive them into such close contact with their own kind, for they are normally most unsociable animals, with each male incessantly on the move in its continual quest for food within the 100 square miles or so of its hunting territory, which includes the smaller territories of two or three females. Their unsocial habits, together with their unusually extensive territorial requirements, must have precluded wolverines from ever being numerous, though the fact that they are rarely seen can be attributed to their perpetual wanderings.

2: Squirrels

Conifer seeds, especially those of spruce, pine, larch and cedar, are a major food of certain mammals and birds, and the cyclic variations in the seed crops of spruce and pine are reflected in regular violent fluctuations in the numbers of some of the conifer forests' inhabitants. Seed production is controlled mainly by weather conditions, though in Eurasia productivity apparently decreases from east to west, for in the eastern taiga 7 good crops are the rule in every 10 years, whereas in the west the ratio falls to 5 in 10; moreover, even in those regions of Scandinavia favorable to pine and spruce, good quantities of seed are only produced at intervals of three or four years, while at higher altitudes poor crops may persist for more than a decade. Total failure of the cone crop follows a cycle of superabundance that exhausts the trees' productive capacity. In northern Europe in particular the immense numbers of cones deposited on the forest floor by the wind, and also by squirrels, woodpeckers and crossbills, form an important source of food for such small rodents as mice, voles and wood lemmings. In peak seed-production years this rodent population, which is potentially capable of bearing successions of litters at very short intervals, may build up to plague proportions and make it possible for the various species of hawks and owls that prey on them to rear exceptionally large broods of young every fourth year or so.

A litter of cone-flakes on a forest path betrays the red squirrel sleeping on a branch above. With its tufted ears and tail of fine hairs curled over its back and projecting an inch in front of its face, it resembles a large hairy fir cone. A shower of flakes falling upon the watcher's upturned face draws his attention to another squirrel with an enormous cone in its mouth. Aligned, motionless, to the bole of the tree, it observes him intently for some minutes with its protuberant beady black eyes, before exploding into lightning activity and scuttering up the tree to a projecting branch, where sitting back against the bole it nibbles at the cone with characteristic desperate urgency, while turning it round and round in its paws with remarkable rapidity. Actually, it manipulates the cone solely with its tiny stubs of thumbs which, unlike its sharp-clawed fingers, have only nails. Abruptly it hurls the cone away, with that febrile irresponsibility of all squirrel actions, to which it is provoked from minute to minute—scratching its head, wagging its tail furiously from side to side, stamping a staccato on the branch while chattering angrily—and then sits forward on the branch to peer at the watcher, before streaking further up the tree on hearing the guttural alarum of another squirrel.

A scrabbling of paws on the rough tinder-dry bark, and a third squirrel whisks up the trunk. Three squirrels a'chasing, with excited squeaks and muffled gutturals, and there is a blaze of color as, each on another's tail, they slither round and round and up and down the trunk, spiraling it so swiftly that the watcher's impression is of a whirling ruddy-gold Catherine-wheel. Suddenly, spontaneously, all three interrupt their erratic convolutions and freeze to the trunk, head downwards, in luxurious abandon, the length of their tautly stretched and widely parted hind legs as if set-pinned, with forepaws hanging free and tails flush with the trunk. For several minutes the three hang motionless, one still holding a large cone in its mouth. How distinctive of squirrels is this instant transition from super-activity to frozen inertia in the most improbable postures; and though such postures can be retained in a gale of wind, despite the burden of a huge cone, even squirrels have been known to fall 80 feet to the forest floor, though typically landing unhurt.

As suddenly and spontaneously, the three are in motion again. One scrabbles up the trunk with extraordinary swiftness to its spiring top, and thence out along the bending clusters of needles, pirouetting on the slenderest twigs, to leap effortlessly over a 12-foot gap to another treetop; and hardly has it alighted, swaying on the outer twigs, before it is twisting half out into space, reaching for a cone. Tearing one off with filed teeth, it swings back to a securer perch on the very tip of the tree; but then scampers all the way down to the ground, and is away in a flash, bounding over the carpet of needles to bury the cone at the base of another tree. However, having scratched a hole, it fills it with needles and places the cone on top! Then it returns to sit on a log and observe the watcher.

It is possible that the flower-buds and seeds of conifers are the staple food of some northern populations of red squirrels, whose range extends right across Eurasia from Ireland to Japan (with an allied race in North America), and from the northern limit of trees south to the Mediterranean and Cambodia; and that the fluctuations in the numbers of those inhabiting spruce forests are regulated by the cropping rhythm of the spruces, for since the squirrels feed both on the flower-buds and on the seeds resulting from these the following year, they experience two consecutive winters of good feeding, enabling them to breed successfully. The Siberian race, distinguished by their blue-gray winter coats, breed exceptionally early in the year after a good cone harvest and produce three litters, each of as many as seven or eight young, in contrast to the single litter of six young normally born by squirrels in northern Europe, and the two litters of those in more southerly latitudes. Furthermore, ample food supplies ensure a lower mortality rate among both young and adults, with the result that the squirrel population under these favourable conditions increases by some 400 per cent. On the other hand when there is a partial or total failure in the cone crop after a peak period, the squirrels breed later in the spring, litters are smaller, losses among the young are very high, and the 75 per cent increase in the population barely equals the overall mortality. Indeed, if in such circumstances large numbers of the previously excessive stock of squirrels die, the population may be reduced to only 1/450 of its previous level.

Siberian squirrels cannot, like birds, emigrate to other countries when the cone harvest fails; but conifer crops in the taiga vary from one region to another, and there are old Russian accounts of mass movements by red squirrels after bad harvests, entailing migrations of 150 or 175 miles into forested tundras, steppes and mountains, with thousands of squirrels meeting their death by drowning while attempting to cross broad rivers. More recent observations confirm these old accounts, with the greater part of one local population of squirrels migrating over a period of two months for several hundred miles from an area where the crop has failed to another where the harvest is good. Though traveling individually at a rate of 2 miles per hour on a front of almost 200 miles, all move in the same direction, crossing rivers up to 4 miles wide. Prior to the decimation of North America's vast eastern forests excessive build-ups in the populations of gray squirrels also resulted in occasional mass dispersals; 500 million of these squirrels were estimated to have migra-

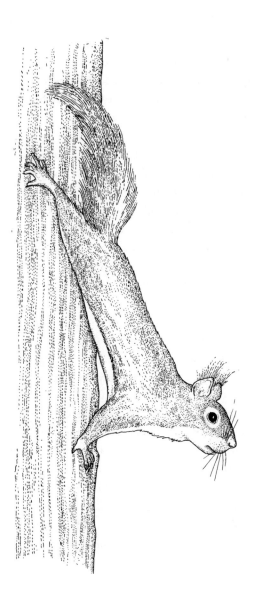

Red squirrel

ted across southern Wisconsin, even crossing the Ohio, in 1843.

Many populations of red squirrels are, however, by no means solely dependent on conifers for food, nor on one kind of conifer for, even in the taiga, larch and Norwegian pine often bear fruit in years when the spruce fails. Nor are they exclusively restricted to coniferous forests. In Britain many inhabit mixed woods, while in Denmark they are believed to have lived continuously in the deciduous forests for 2,000 or 3,000 years. A suitable habitat must, however, include a certain proportion of mature woodland that will provide not only cone seed but also trees—preferably Scots pine more than fifteen years old—sufficiently developed to hold the football-sized woven mass of twigs, grass, moss and shredded bark (often of honeysuckle) of which the dreys are built. Some of these are used as shelters in the winter and others, lined with similar materials and perhaps sheep's wool, as nests for the young for a couple of months after birth.

British red squirrels have in fact a very wide range of seasonal foods, and it is hard to credit that any squirrel ever has sufficient patience to strip enough cones of their scales to make an adequate meal on the seeds alone, since 200 cones contain less than half an ounce of seed. Moreover, opening up a cone is a skilled operation that young squirrels only learn to perform by practice, just as they ultimately learn by trial and error that the quickest way to open a nut is by chiseling into the natural grooves in the shell. One wonders how many squirrels break the incisor teeth with which they chisel, for if one of these is lost the opposing tooth has nothing to grind against, with the result that its owner must eventually die of starvation or from the effect of the tooth growing in a curve unimpeded until it finally pierces the skull.

In the spring, according to Monica Shorten—to whose monograph on the red squirrel I am indebted—squirrels feed on the buds and shoots of young conifers, bulbs, roots and some insects, and later in the spring on pine seed; while from April to June when sap, with its high sugar content, is flowing up young conifers, and also when it recedes in July, the squirrels gnaw off the bark in order to tap the sap in the cambium layer between the bark and the newest wood, and also chew and swallow the cambium itself. The incidence of "barking" is liable to increase in dry weather, when drinking water is scarce, and result in young trees being killed if a ring of bark is stripped off near the base. The most favored trees are Scots pines 20 to 40 feet high and from 15 to 40 years old, though larch and spruce are also tapped; while gray squirrels usually select deciduous trees from 8 to 40 years old. The latter are, incidentally, able to distinguish between the acorns—their main food—of different species of oak, possibly favoring those with a higher content of sugar and less of tannin. American red squirrels also tap maples and black birches in the spring, either lapping the sap from a natural break or gnawing saucer-shaped hollows in the upper side of a branch into which the sap flows.

Squirrels are not the only exploiters of sap. The North American sap-sucker, a woodpecker, chisels out rings of holes around the bole of a tree as sap catchers, and these are poached by acorn-woodpeckers. Porcupines and badgers are sap addicts, and it is possible that cambium contains essential mineral traces, for black bears, on emerging from hibernation in the northern Rockies, habitually bite large chunks of bark out of lodge-pole pines, and one pine in every ten may be barked in some districts; while in Washington State bark is peeled from second-growth Douglas firs. Victor Calahane believes that the cambium of various kinds of pines possesses tonic properties, and this belief is shared by the countryfolk of Bulgaria, where brown bears also regularly strip the bark from pine trees, ringing them to a considerable height, after coming out of hibernation.

But, to return to the extensive seasonal diet of red squirrels, this is supplemented in the summer by wild fruits, flowers and berries, large numbers of insect larvae, various fungi (including the most deadly poisonous), and some birds' eggs and nestlings; while during the late summer and fall, when there is a super-abundance of such foods as acorns, sweet chestnuts, beechmast, cone and plant seed, hazel nuts, hips and haws, agarics and truffles, squirrels are feverishly active in collecting, burying and storing these. But European red squirrels do not normally amass large hoards in the manner of American red and pine squirrels, which dump green cones in "middens" that may, reputedly, be 2 or 3 feet deep, as much as 30 feet in diameter, and contain from 3 to 10 bushels of the current year's crop of cones. Moreover each squirrel is said to own several of these middens, which are usually piled up around a stump or log in a central part of its territory, and in a damp place, since the moisture, instead of rotting the cones, prevents them from opening and losing their seeds. Despite the labor involved in the collection of such extraordinary numbers of cones, some California pine squirrels subsequently distribute the contents of their middens in smaller caches under stones, leaves or bark, or in uncovered holes, or even in springs or running water, from which they may not be removed and eaten until two years later. Indeed William T. Shaw has described finding a store of 2,479 sequoia cones, the majority of which were still in good condition after three years' submersion, in a large number of caches in the moist tract of a spring-head. Such stores must prove valuable if the cone harvest fails in subsequent years.

In America and Siberia the squirrels also gather fungi throughout the summer and dry them under bark or by impaling them on the ends of branches, before caching them in middles. G. A. Hardy, however, writing in the *Canadian Field Naturalist*, describes finding fifty-nine fungi of thirteen different species stored in six small cavities in a very dry stump of an old Douglas fir in a British Columbia forest; and this would appear to be a more suitable site for such water-absorbent material than damp middens.

European squirrels either bury their small hoards of nuts, acorns or beechmast or, more usually, cache them in old dreys, and these hoards often remain untouched throughout the winter, when the squirrels obtain the bulk of their food on the forest floor. Although essentially arboreal, squirrels frequently descend to ground level to forage, to drink in hot weather, and when migrating from one stand of conifers to another. Nevertheless, although the various locations of buried hoards appear to be forgotten by their owners, they probably serve a purpose because, contrary to popular belief, squirrels do not hibernate. In a mild winter indeed the period from autumn to New Year is one of maximum activity, and there is even some evidence that their populations increase, rather than decrease, after a series of severe winters. They may be inactive for short periods during spells of continuous gales or heavy snow because of the difficulty they experience in moving around; but they cannot survive for longer than a few days without food. In January 1945 they were active in Switzerland in temperatures of 5 degrees F with snow lying 20 inches deep; while in 1947, when there was unbroken frost for fifty-six consecutive days after the New Year in the central Highlands of Scotland they were abroad in temperatures as low as minus 10 and minus 15 degrees. It is in these conditions perhaps that some squirrels lose considerable portions of their tails, though this accident does not make them less mobile. During these winter excursions the squirrels rediscover their hoards, or chance upon those of other squirrels, and are apparently able to scent these under several inches of snow. A proportion of those fruits that are never found germinate and grow into trees, though probably not of the kind intended by the forester!

3: Wood Borers and Honeydew Collectors

The actual floor of a pine forest has little to offer its inhabitants, even in the summer. Lacking sunlight, vegetation grows only sparsely or not at all on the poor soil, deficient in lime and organic materials. The tawny carpet of rotting needles decays only slowly because their tough skins and resinous content are resistant to bacteria, while beneath this acid carpet the pale-gray topsoil, or podzol, is leached of what minerals it holds by surface water draining downwards. In the absence of earthworms and effective action by bacteria it is the fungi that are the primary agents in breaking down and decomposing the layer of needles. In the late summer and autumn coniferous woods display an incomparable wealth and color of fungi—brown, white, lilac, green, pale-purple, red and orange, black, yellow, tangerine and especially the mottled bright scarlet of the poisonous, though not deadly fly agaric; and it has been estimated that a cubic foot of podzol and its covering of needles may contain 3,000 miles of microscopic interwoven fungal threads or mycelium.

Cellulose, the basis of wood, is also so tough and resistant that it cannot be destroyed by the natural processes of decay, but only by such specialized agents as that extraordinary animal the goat, by snails, the larvae of some wood-boring beetles, termites and fungi. Fungi capable of breaking down dead wood usually produce large fruiting bodies such as mushrooms and toadstools above ground, and the tips of the growing hyphae, the tubular threads of the mycelium, secrete an enzyme or chemical ferment which gradually dissolves the cellulose in the wood's millions of dead cells. But the mycelium also apparently influences the growth of living trees, for there is a close association between certain trees and certain fungi—*Boletus elegans* and larch, the orange-cap boletus and birch, and the fly agaric with both birch and pine; and seedlings of pine and spruce, growing wild in newly drained peat-bogs, thrive normally only when infected with mycelium; uninfected seedlings suffer from nitrogen starvation and eventually die. The mycelium, matted around the tiny roots, probably acts like root hairs, passing water and other material to the trees.

In Europe and Siberia spruce forests are less hostile to life than pine woods, for they are often boggy, with an undergrowth of juniper, dwarf willow and wild rosebushes, all thickly intertwined with bindweed, together with almost pure stretches of bilberry. While it is difficult to credit that a square yard of Swedish spruce forest may be the habitat of 2 million insects and spiders, many invertebrates continue active during the winter months, when the canopy of snow overlaying the trees creates a micro-climate of relative warmth beneath, and provide food for the insatiable appetites of such small rodents as shrews. Insects must play a major role in the growth and decay of coniferous forests. It is true that comparatively few species feed on conifers, though many kinds of seed-wasps or chalchids do so extensively on non-resinous seeds. It has been suggested that the resinous flavour and sticky nature of a conifer's bark and needles render them unpalatable to insects, and that this also constitutes a form of protection against herbivores; though roe deer, hares and rabbits do not appear to dislike sapling conifers. However, those insects that do exploit this niche are able to do so in large numbers, feeding on every product of the trees. The caterpillars of the pine saw-fly, for example, strip the needles from entire branches of Scots pine, while pine weevils, eating into the bark of younger branches in order to gain access to the more edible underlying tissues, are particularly destructive to Scots pines by interrupting the normal flow of the sap. Pine procession caterpillars may defoliate a tree, though apparently without causing permanent damage to it. Living communally in squirming masses in large silk-spun envelopes, these caterpillars periodically migrate in search of food on other parts of the tree, or descend to the ground to travel over the forest floor in single file, head to tail along a silken thread spun by the leading caterpillar and, if arranged in a ring, continue to circulate in an endless chain until exhausted. One wonders why it is more advantageous to travel in single file than, like the oak procession caterpillars, in single file at the head of the column, in twos further back, and then in threes and fours up to six or seven deep, before eventually tailing off into single file again!

And then there are the wood borers: the spruce-bark beetles, ambrosia beetles and longicorns, of which there are no fewer than sixty species in Britain alone; the timberman, with antennae four times as long as its body acting as receptors to pick up the scent of females, and extended like calipers when it settles on a felled pine; and the two-toothed bark beetles, whose star-shaped gallery systems, gnawed out of the surface wood of pine and spruce branches, are arranged around a central chamber in which the male mates with a number of females, each of whom tunnels her own main gallery leading from this chamber. For these wood borers a conifer provides both habitation and food source, though some borers apparently obtain no nutriment from the wood itself, either subsisting on the starch and sugar contained in its cells or secreting enzymes that convert the wood by chemical action into nutritive substances. Ambrosia beetles or pinhole borers—of which there are some 400 species—and wood wasps obtain their food in a different way. The female ambrosia, having gnawed a cylindrical burrow rarely exceeding the diameter of a stout pin in unseasoned wood, prepares a layer of "sawdust" and excreta on which she cultivates a mold that stains the walls of the burrow and serves as food for her larvae. If she is removed from the burrow it is soon invaded by alien fungi. Many kinds of fungi would not be able to infect trees if they were not introduced by boring insects and subsequently spread by contaminated larvae when tunneling; and it is a beetle-fungi association that is mainly responsible for Dutch elm disease, as a result of an engraver beetle infecting an elm with a fungus (*Ceratostomella*) when feeding on young branches or boring tunnels in which to lay eggs. When the larvae emerge in the spring, after wintering under the bark, they are contaminated both internally and externally with spores of this fungus.

The splendid inch-long wood wasps or horntails—the orange and black *Sirex gigas* and the blue *Sirex cyaneus*—exploit most of the conifers, laying their eggs in holes drilled with their needle-like ovipositors in the solid wood of dead or dying trees, and sometimes in living trees, despite the fact that the saw-edged blades of their ovipositors are liable to become trapped in the contracting fibers of green wood. A pair of glands at the base of the ovipositor contain the fruiting bodies or conidia of a fungus, which are extruded with the eggs and subsequently develop into a crop of mold on the walls of the burrow, affording either

direct food for the larvae or acting on the wood to make it di-
gestible. After hatching, the larvae gnaw their way through
twisting tunnels up to 12 inches long for a period of 2½ to 3
years, before finally stopping to pupate when within ½ inch or 1
inch of the tree's outer skin.

The wood borers are preyed upon by other boring insects.
The eggs, larvae and pupae of the two-toothed beetles are de-
voured by ant-beetles, and the wood wasps are parasited by the
ichneumon wasps. In June and July the bluish-black and white
ichneumon searches for the wood wasps' larvae, systematically
exploring tree trunks with the tips of her antennae and possibly
scenting the grubs. On locating one she displays every evidence
of excitement before beginning to bore into the trunk. Arching
her body on her red legs into the semblance of a drilling-plat-
form to support her 1½-inch-long, toothed and bristle-like ovipositor (¼ inch longer than her body) she drills a hole 1¼ inches
deep in the solid wood in less than twenty minutes. However,
like the wood wasps, she may make the mistake of boring into
living wood and become entrapped by her ovipositor or, having
completed her drilling, fail to locate the grub which may perhaps have burrowed deeper, though deceiving the ichneumon
by lingering traces of its odor; but if the burrow is occupied,
the ichneumon extrudes her eggs through a central duct in her
ovipositor into the larva, on which her own larvae will feed
when they hatch.

The most obvious inhabitants of the pine forest are the wood
ants, predominantly *Formica rufa*, and as many as five or six of
their rounded, cone-shaped "hills" may be sited along a front of
a few score yards of fencing stobs, at the base of pine trees, or at
the edges of glades or especially of needle-strewn paths.
Thatched with dead pine needles, small twigs and other detri-

tus, the hills vary in size from small cushions to relatively gigantic structures 27 feet in circumference at the base and 4 feet in
depth above ground; in the taiga indeed some are large enough
to furnish brown bears with winter quarters. Such structures
may have been occupied for forty years or more and house
perhaps 100,000 ants, for they include subterranean labyrinths
of inter-communicating chambers, with access to the exterior of
the hill through galleries and numbers of entrances, which are
guarded by sentinels and closed with twigs at night by the
workers. A large colony of *Formica rufa* includes numerous
queens, in contrast to colonies of most other ants and termites;
and these, instead of setting off to found their own colonies after
the mating flight, normally return to their native hill or to those
of other *rufa* ants, though a minority are successful in gaining
entry to the hills of their relatives, the *fusca* ants, without being
repulsed or killed. In this event it is the intruder who becomes
the queen of a hybrid colony, and new pure stocks of *rufa* ants
can only be established when a number of queens, accompanied
by a retinue of workers, emigrate from their native hill.

The orange-brown hills of the wood ants are the most conspicuous feature of the pine woods. Throughout the winter their
inmates remain within their fortress, though a few sluggish individuals are always to be found in the soft dry mold within a
quarter of an inch of the outer covering of pine needles; but on a
mild and humid day in March the tops of those hills from which
the snow has melted swarm with ants, and a few may be observed moving lethargically about the undergrowth within a foot
or two of the hill. According to John Sudd, the first act of the
newly stirring workers is to carry out the grains of detritus that
percolated the hill during the winter. Then, the outer thatch is
attended to; and even in March workers are already repairing a
torn or rent thatch, transporting needles, flakes of cones and

other material to the snow-flattened dome. Needles up to an inch long are carried in the ants' jaws, while the larger "twigs" are pulled by an ant at one end and pushed by another at the other end, with perhaps a third manipulating the mid-portion. Yet it is impossible to observe any planned working rhythm among the seething mass of ants, except that those leaving the hill do so with empty jaws, while those arriving are carrying material. Though a creditable job is made of these early repairs, the thatch remains jagged and layered, lacking the smooth overall finish of the perfect hill, obtained by an incessant turning and re-turning of the thatch, to which additions are still being made in May. A smooth thatch is apparently of great importance, possibly as a preventative against damage by heavy rain, though more probably it acts as an insulator; for by constantly working it the ants can no doubt regulate the temperature within the hill. Certainly, the temperature at the surface fluctuates greatly according to the time of day, whereas within the nest it becomes much more equable as the depth increases, and Sudd has suggested that the pupae can be "forced" in the very high daytime temperatures prevailing at the top of the nest.

On a warm April day of blue skies, when the dead pine cones are crackling, the seed-pods of the broom are popping in the hot sun, and the woods are filled with the soft twittering and merry jingoes of siskins pricked with gold, the top of a sunny hill seethes with ants, though deep within the woods the inhabitants of shaded hills are still sluggish and mainly interred. But by mid-June, when the pine woods are redolent with the sun-dried tindery aroma of summer, and the first jewel-like males of the red damsel-flies dart up and down the sunny rides through the woods, these late awakeners have joined the endless patrols of ants on the march along the highways of springy brown peat that radiate for scores of yards—more than 100 yards in some instances—from the hills, from which tens of thousands of workers are pouring out. Each colony uses its own highways and maintains its own food territory. These highways are usually very straight and as bare of needles as beaten-earth floors, for some ants are constantly engaged in "sweeping" them, immediately pulling away any needle that falls on them, though it is not clear whether these ants are sweepers only or chance passers-by when a needle falls. Even the vegetation bordering the highways may be cut down as a further measure to keeping them clean, while large twigs, stones and pits are undermined or circuited, though none of these obstacles cause much delay or confusion among the endless processions.

The busiest highways lead to the tallest pine trees, up and down whose rough-barked trunks, to a height at which they can no longer be followed with binoculars, pass in continual succession two streams of ants. None of the descending ants carry any obvious spoils, for the good reason that they have been "milking" aphids of their honeydew—the highly nutritious excreta of these plant-lice—which may comprise more than 60 per cent of their food. Wood ants milk some sixty-five kinds of aphids, and they are so numerous and well-armed with sharp mandibles and the equipment to squirt formic acid to a distance of 6 or 12 inches, that few other insects venture on to their aphid trees and the population of saw-flies in an ant wood is much reduced. In German coniferous forests, however, both *Formica rufa* and a bee, *Apis mellifera*, collect honeydew. Although the ants keep the bees away from their trees with their "spray-guns," the bees gather honeydew surplus to the ants' requirements from leaves, and on hot days when the ants remain within their hills; and since aphids are more numerous in trees near ant-hills, the yield of honey from an ant-inhabited forest is more than 1½ times as great as in a forest without ants. The wood ants also feed on sap, resin and very small quantities of seeds, fungi and carrion; but their secondary food consists of insects, and a large colony may bring into the nest 100,000 insects a day in favorable weather conditions.

Woodpeckers appear to be the wood ants' only significant predators, especially the great black woodpeckers which inhabit all extensive coniferous forests in Europe as far north as the tree line, and feed mainly on ants during the winter, foraging several miles to obtain these, and locating their hills even when these are buried under 3 feet of snow. Woodpeckers are major controllers of ant populations and also of wood-boring insects, and are extremely successful birds. Marvelously adapted to their specialized roles, they have colonized almost every part of the world, with the notable exceptions of Australia and Madagascar in which their niche is filled by other species. In Europe the majority prefer mixed forests, in which deciduous trees outnumber conifers. However, four out of the ten species of European woodpeckers are predominantly inhabitants of coniferous forests, and in Finland the greater spotted or pied woodpeckers feed almost exclusively on spruce and pine seed during the winter months. In the course of an eleven-hour day one woodpecker can open as many as 137 cones and extract about 900 seeds from these with beak and tongue, after breaking off the scales; displaying considerable ingenuity in wedging the cones in cracks or, after repeated failures, chiseling the latter to the correct size. Only at the end of April or early in May, when the cones have opened in the hot sun and the seeds have fallen to the ground, do these Finnish woodpeckers revert to a diet of spiders and the larvae and pupae of ants, whereas those of the British race feed almost exclusively on larvae all the year round, and pines and larches worked by them are invariably infested with longicorns and other boring beetles. Thus the failure of the cone crop in Scandinavian forests results in extensive dispersals of these northern woodpeckers to other parts of Europe.

For the purpose of winkling out ants and wood-boring grubs, after first hacking away the bark in long strips and then chiseling into the galleries, the spear-like horny tip of a woodpecker's beak is equipped with numerous small barbs, and its tongue coated with a sticky mucus discharged from large salivary glands. The green woodpecker, which specializes in wood ants and red ants, can indeed shoot out its tongue 4 inches beyond the tip of its beak and manipulate it in any direction when probing for ants in twisting bark crevices or in rotten tree stumps. A woodpecker's beak can be operated with the delicacy of a Morse-code operator when drumming out its staccato mating call that reverberates through the woods, or with the efficiency of a cold-chisel when hacking out its nesting-hole. According to Heinz Sielmann, who made a unique field study and photographic record of several species of woodpeckers in a forest of Westphalia, and to whose observations I am much indebted, the crow-sized black woodpecker—which is replaced in North America by the very similar pileated woodpecker—drums 500 or 600 times a day on dry branches as near as possible to the top of a tree, when advertising his presence to a prospective mate, while clinging to the tree with his claws. With two claws aligned up the trunk, one down it, and one projecting sideways, he obtains a sure grip on the smoothest bole, while the upper part of his body, inclined backwards at a steep angle, is supported by the stiff tapering feathers of his tail. At the peak of his excitement he may drum ten times a minute at the rate of 6 to 10 strokes a second, while a pied woodpecker, little larger than a starling, strikes at the rate of 12 to 14 strokes in less than a second. That a woodpecker's skull can withstand such a shock-rate is due to the fact that every blow with the beak is absorbed by the spongy

Pileated woodpecker

and elastic tissue or flexible cartilage that connects the root of the beak to the bones of the skull, which are not rigidly joined, as in the case of other birds.

Still more severe jarring has to be withstood when a woodpecker is excavating its nesting-hole. A black woodpecker, for example, must deliver from 3 to 15 beak blows to hack off a wood chip not more than ¼ inch or at most 1¼ inches long, while a male pied hammers away for an hour at a time and for as much as six hours a day to excavate a hole 11 to 12 inches deep and 5 inches in diameter after three weeks' work. According to Sielmann, black woodpeckers prefer to excavate their nesting-holes 18 inches deep and 10 inches in diameter, in hard, sound beechwood: whereas green woodpeckers, whose beaks are not as powerful as those of other species, excavate their holes in rotten wood or adapt the holes of other woodpeckers. Both male and female black woodpeckers share in excavation, and begin by chiseling out wedge-shaped chips:

> Their rhythm and technique are quite different from those used in drumming. During drumming a woodpecker bends his head back as a preliminary to furiously fast bursts of drumming, with his neck outstretched and his beak kept close to the tree trunk. But when tunnelling, the bird uses the swing of neck and head. Holding himself fast to the tree with his claws, he bends the upper part of his body back slightly to put the greatest possible force behind every swing of his . . . powerful . . . beak, extending and deepening the hole horizontally by hammering with head aslant, first from the right and then from the left.

Where woodpeckers are numerous they play an important role in influencing the general ecology of a forest, for their nesting-holes, both old and new, attract a remarkable variety of other birds and also mammals. The 1,250-acre mixed forest of beech, oak, larch and pine, surrounded by young plantations, in which Sielmann worked, was so rich in old timber that in many parts ageing trees were allowed to stand until storms brought them down. This was an ideal sanctuary for woodpeckers, of which 3 pairs of black, 6 pairs of pied and 2 pairs of green were present. Their holes, and those of their predecessors, provided nesting accommodation for no fewer than 20 pairs of jackdaws and 10 pairs of stockdoves, in addition to starlings, nuthatches, tits, pied flycatchers, hoopoes and goldeneye ducks, and were also used by bats and dormice and as dreys by red squirrels for their young.

4: Crossbills and Other Birds of the Coniferous Forests

The insect population of the coniferous forests is exploited during the summer months by a host of immigrant birds from more southerly latitudes, which nest in the forests and raise their young on a diet of insects and their larvae. Song thrushes, for example, nest in the company of Siberian tits and jays, and also red squirrels, in the most northerly pine forest in Europe on the seventieth parallel in Norway; though it is true that this forest also includes birches and willows, for while the coniferous forests of Scandinavia are dominated by spruce, these are replaced further north by pine and birch, and at polar limits by birch only. But few insectivorous species winter in these northern forests. Siskins and redpolls, nesting and feeding in the high tops of spruces, pines and larches, move out to the birch and alder country in the winter. Waxwings disperse south and west in search of berries, especially those of the mountain ash. Bramblings emigrate in the autumn to the arable lands and deciduous woods of more southerly regions, to feed on grain and especially beechmast, and assemble in millions in localities where mast is plentiful: 11 million being reported in one district in Switzerland in the winter of 1946–7, and 72 million in another in 1950–1.

The birds that winter in the coniferous forests include tree-creepers, goldcrests, tits, black-capped chicadees, grosbeaks, crossbills, crows and woodpeckers, the predatory hawks and owls, and oddly enough four kinds of grouse—capercaillie, black grouse, hazel-hen and willow grouse. Of these only about fifty species are equipped to feed on and digest the unnutritious products of the conifers. Grouse, however, can digest with equal facility the needles, buds and shoots of pine, spruce and larch, though the nutritive content of these is so low that during the winter the great capercaillie must, like the American blue grouse, feed almost continuously through the short hours of daylight in order to take in a sufficient bulk of needles. In the summer, however, all these grouse feed extensively on the berries of the shrubs associated with the coniferous forest—crow-berry, bilberry, raspberry, bramble, hip and mountain ash.

Crested tits vary their diet of pine seed and hibernating and pupating insects with juniper berries. The pine grosbeaks (which range almost as far north as the Arctic Circle) employ their thick beaks, assisted by powerful neck muscles, to batter open spruce cones; but they also feed on the seeds of birch, willow and heather, and in Sweden are more often in the birch woods than the coniferous forest. In eastern Europe the nut-cracker crows make similar use of their hard beaks to obtain seeds by hammering the cones of pines or cedars to pieces, aided in this by a notch in the upper mandible. They specialize in the seeds of the arolla pine. These weigh about ⅓ gram in comparison with the less than 1/100 gram of most conifer seeds, and the arolla's total yield of seed is from 30,000 to 300,000 times as great as that of other conifers. However, nutcrackers also inhabit coniferous forests in Sweden where there are no arolla pines, and there rely for the bulk of their food on hazel nuts, fruits and berries obtained outside the forest. Like the Siberian jays that subsist during the northern winter on their caches of cedar nuts, which they apparently have the prescience to bury in places where snow will lie less deeply, the nutcrackers also bury large quantities of food that they collect during a period of several weeks in the autumn over an area of 3 or 4 miles, and are subsequently successful in relocating their caches and digging them up daily during the winter. By what means they are able to find these stores, with only a very small percentage of error, when the ground is covered with 18 inches of snow, remains a mystery.

Among the most specialized and the most dependent on the products of conifers are crossbills—the parrot crossbills of the Scottish Highlands and northern Europe, and the common or red crossbills and the white-winged or two-barred crossbills of North America and Eurasia. So specialized are they that eggs are laid as early as the end of February or before the middle of March to ensure that the nestlings hatch when ample supplies of food are available in the form of spruce, pine and larch seeds; for these are most easily obtained from the hard cones when these begin to open in the increasingly hot sun of spring and early summer. Such an early nesting may involve the incubating hen-bird being fed on the nest by the cock in very cold weather, or the nest on its foundation of twigs being covered with 7 or 8 inches of snow, though this does not prevent the eggs from hatching. Moreover the parents are able to leave newly hatched young in order to collect food in temperatures as low as zero degrees F, because the nestlings are resistant to cold, lapsing during their mother's absence into a temporary state of coma, from which they are immediately revived by the warmth of her body when she returns to brood them. Their resistance contrasts with the vulnerability of young capercaillies which hatch in June and, during their early weeks, are in constant need of

Common or red crossbill

the hen's warmth. Prolonged periods of low temperatures at this season may result in them freezing to death or being unable to obtain food; and these hazards are reflected in the fluctuating numbers of caper.

Crossbills are also equipped with specialized beaks, whose powerful arched mandibles are crossed at their tips, though this peculiarity only becomes obvious when they are within a few feet of the observer. Extra-strong jaw muscles enable a crossbill to exert a pressure of 100 pounds to the square inch at the cutting edges of its mandibles and shear through the tough scales of a pine cone. There is no general agreement as to the actual technique involved. According to some observers the crossed mandibles have no special significance, because the cone is opened by a sideways movement of the lower mandible. According to others, the upper mandible bears down laterally on the space between cone and scale and forces them apart; and since the crossed tips do not meet, a shearing action is obtained, enabling the long tongue to penetrate to the seed and withdraw it, whereas most birds cannot extract the seeds until the cones open naturally, though siskins exploit cones previously opened by crossbills.

It is generally held that the differing beaks of the three species of crossbills have been developed to deal with different types of cones. Thus, the markedly heavy beak of the parrot crossbill can cope with the thick hard scales of pine cones, the much lighter beak of the common crossbill with the softer and less resistant spruce cones, and the still finer beak of the white-winged crossbill with those of larch and also spruce and stone-pine; but, while theoretically plausible, these distinctions do not hold good in practice, for the parrot crossbills of the Scottish Highlands are equally partial to spruce and larch cones, while the main food supply of the immigrant common crossbills consists of pine cones. Parrot crossbills indeed ignore young pine cones in favor of young larch cones, and if the Highland crop of larch cones is a heavy one, then this is their primary source of food, with pine cones as a secondary source.

By Christmas a flock of as many as sixty parrot crossbills may be exploiting a single grove of larches, feeding daily high up in the trees, in company with goldcrests and coal tits and perhaps a red squirrel. Being extremely acrobatic, they are able to penetrate the densest foliage in their search for cones, and swinging from the branches or hanging upside down from supple twig ends, they nip or wrench off the small cones very easily and neatly by their stalks. Then they carry them to nearby branches and, standing on them with both feet, twist and gouge out the seeds. (Their technique has been contrasted with that of the white-winged crossbills, which extract the seeds from larch cones while clinging tit-like beneath them and without nipping them off; but in fact parrot crossbills do not sever young larch cones, but dig out the seeds from the tops of the cones.) Nevertheless, a high proportion of both larch and pine cones are apparently too hard even for parrot crossbills to open, and their tremendously energetic and rapid method of feeding appears to be extremely wasteful, since multitudes of these cones are prematurely dropped, even hurled down, intact almost as soon as they have been nipped off; whereas a single spruce cone may be worked at for ten minutes or even half an hour, as the crossbill twists the scales off. The woody impact of falling larch cones on hard surfaces and their dull thuds on the ground beneath a feeding flock of crossbills is continuous.

Their industry is prodigious, though their chirping calls seldom cease for an instant, and their feeding is interrupted only for a brief bar of song from the tip of a spiring larch, or an excursion to a nearby lime tree to sip raindrops off the leaves, for crossbills drink often. On some days they feed confidently within 6 or 10 feet of an observer; on other occasions they are shy and restless, with the whole flock rising from the larches time and again, to the accompaniment of a sudden crescendo of their melodious twittering, to circle round high above the grove, before darting down to resume feeding again or to depart, with characteristic jingle of "sleigh-bells," for another larch grove or pine wood a mile or more distant.

It is on the seeds of the young green larch cones that the young crossbills are fed when they fledge in April and May; and each parent, hanging upside down from the feathery green fronds, feeds one or two, or two or three, members of the brood independently. By the end of June, when they have already been on the wing for several weeks, some of the fledglings are beginning to twist at the stalks of cones and wrench them off; but though a single seed-flake may be swallowed, the cones are quickly dropped in apparent disgust, and they still seem unable, or unwilling, to feed themselves. Thus, in a fine summer, larch groves and pine woods are noisy the day long with the incessant pleading *vee-tew*, *vee-tew* of these young crossbills, as hour after hour they pester their parents to feed them, with different members of the brood following their respective parents from branch to branch. Yet the latter pay little attention to their begging, only infrequently alighting beside one to regurgitate a milky fluid with which a cock will also feed his mate on a frosty winter's day. Despite their apparently improvident method of feeding, a quarter-acre of pine wood appears to provide an inexhaustible supply of seeds in the summer. Within a few minutes of a family's arrival the ground below the trees is littered with a couple of hundred cones and a single cock, feeding only one fledgling, may drop 28 cones in 20 minutes, while in the course of a single evening 6 parents with their families are capable of stripping 500 cones from 2 pine trees.

Although the parrot crossbills of the Scottish Highlands are permanently resident, all three species of crossbill are more or less nomadic over most of their range, according to the relative abundance of cones in a particular year. When poor crops of cones persist over a number of years parrot crossbills are sparsely distributed over northern Europe. An abundant harvest of cones, on the other hand, results in correspondingly large numbers of young crossbills. But if this good harvest is followed by a poor one, then the surplus stock must emigrate in search of more productive forests; while total failure accounts for those sporadic mass dispersals of mainly immature crossbills from their native forests. Such dispersals fan out in random directions and carry the participants far beyond the limits of their normal specific range; but although breeding colonies may be founded in these new lands, these usually die out after two or three generations.

Their distribution may also be affected by other factors. Parrot and common crossbills, for example, have to compete for food with pied woodpeckers and red squirrels. Moreover, all three species appear to be mutually antagonistic. Parrot crossbills are never known to breed in numbers in proximity to common crossbills, while in the Canadian Arctic, where there is a considerable overlap in the ranges of the common and white-winged races, these too rarely breed in proximity, since the former tend to evacuate their territories in favor of the latter.

5: Hoarders and Hibernators

Although deciduous forests range from regions of sub-tropical heat to those of near-arctic cold they are typical of the temperate zone and provide a rich harvest of seeds, buds, insects and caterpillars for birds and mammals. The summer bird population of an English deciduous woodland may indeed reach a density of 1,500 or even 2,000 birds to 100 acres, compared with less than 100 birds to this acreage in a wood on a Scottish island or in one of the primeval northern forests. A single oak tree may be ravaged by 50,000 caterpillars, while the astronomical numbers of aphids feeding on the sap of the oak leaves provide numerous birds and insects with a primary source of food in the summer, as do their eggs in the winter. Clear a forest of its fallen logs and decaying timber, and almost a quarter of its potential insect species is lost. Every type of food is exploited by one species of bird or another. Hawfinches, which rear their nestlings on insects, feed on dry seeds such as beechmast in the winter, on buds in the spring, and on the kernels of fruit stones in the autumn, exerting pressures of from 60 to 90 pounds at the tips of their beaks to crack the stones. Bullfinches nip off the buds of fruit trees at the rate of thirty a minute. Nuthatches, woodpeckers, woodpigeons, and European jays gorge on the abundant crops of oak acorns and, by hoarding them, influence the growth of forests.

The jays bury their acorns in the ground singly and at random, thereby preserving them because these fruits cannot survive prolonged exposure to drought or frost while lying on the surface. Carrying one acorn in its beak and another one or two or three in its gullet, a jay transports these for half a mile or more to a piece of relatively open ground, and buries them in crevices or under dead leaves, though occasionally one excavates a hole with its beak and, disgorging an acorn into it, hammers it in and covers it up. About a week after the jays have concluded caching operations they begin to dig up their hoards. That they bury more than they will find again in the course of the winter is indicated by one estimate that 300,000 acorns may be taken by jays from a single German oak wood, though when the acorns germinate and sprout above the ground in the spring, the jays dig up some of these seedlings before all the nourishment in the fruit has been exhausted. However, a proportion of those that they do not find grow into trees, and the ability of jays to establish new oak forests can be judged by the fact that 50 per cent of Czechoslovakia's existing pine forests have been colonized by an under-story of oak trees derived from their buried acorns.

The creation of a new wood or forest is of course a long-term operation by natural processes, and the interval between the germination of an embryo tree and its maturity spans many generations of birds and rodents, for though a coppiced oak is capable of bearing acorns after 25 years, the tree does not come into full production for a further 15 years and, like the beech, does not carry maximum crops until it is 70 or 80 years old. And what is this period of growth in comparison with the 2,000 or 3,000 years of a redwood, the 4,500 or 5,000 years of a bristlecone pine, or the 12,000 years of a huckleberry shrub or Australian cycad! That the California redwoods are able to survive to such ages may be because their bark contains an antibiotic that inhibits the growth of lichens, mosses and other plants likely to colonize their trunks, thus rendering them resistant to the occasional ground fires, which are unable to spread upwards without the aid of a corridor of tinder-dry lichens.

Long-tailed wood and deer mice chisel into the hardest nuts with incisors that never wear down because they are continually growing, and shrews snout about in a deep leaf-litter and topsoil for dormant insects and the pupae of caterpillars that have fallen from the trees; or, like the North American short-tailed shrews, are themselves predators, killing mice twice their own weight with a swift-acting poison, secreted by their salivary glands, which flows into the wound inflicted by the long incisors of their lower jaws and, with effects very similar to cobra poison, retard the animal's heart action and breathing. Since shrews are afflicted with a very high metabolic rate—the cause of their ex-

Short-tailed shrew

treme pugnacity—they are driven to consume between three-quarters and one and a half times their own weight in food every twenty-four hours, resting for only the briefest intervals. If prevented from feeding they die within twelve hours and, since they do not hibernate, comparatively few survive the winter.

The early deaths of many other small mammals, including mice, are attributable to this inability to maintain body heat when adequate quantities of food are not continually available. Indeed the only rodent in temperate regions regularly to hibernate, instead of feeding throughout the winter or subsisting on food caches, is the dormouse, which can do so for periods of from three to seven months according to the climatic conditions prevailing in its particular locality. In Britain a dormouse's hibernatory period is determined by the availability of food, not by weather conditions. If fruit, nuts and berries are abundant in the autumn it can put on enough fat to retreat into a cavity under the roots of a tree or into another rodent's old burrow before the end of September; but if food supplies are less abundant hibernation may be postponed until early in November. In its hibernaculum the dormouse's temperature falls to around 39 degrees F, or to a level slightly above that of its surroundings, and its heart rate, respiration and metabolism are correspondingly reduced. As an additional protective measure in severe winters, with temperatures falling below freezing point, its heart-beat quickens, heat production is increased and its body temperature is stabilized at a degree or so above freezing point. However, the act of hibernating does not necessarily ensure an animal's survival during the winter, for if temperatures continue to fall the dormouse wakes up and, if it is unable to move to a warmer place, freezes to death. On the other hand a mild winter can also prove fatal, for during an unseasonably warm spell the dormouse may wake up and, as its temperature rapidly rises to normal, become active; but, unable to find food, it uses up its reserves of fat prematurely and dies of starvation.

I cannot recall any estimate of the effects on deciduous woodlands of mice and voles which eat large numbers of tree seedlings before these can develop, and thus prevent natural regeneration. It may be that such regeneration is only possible in peak years of acorn and beechmast crops, particularly if these coincide with lows in the cycle of rodent numbers. But if the influence of mice and voles on woodlands is an unknown factor, there is no doubt of their essential role in the forest community as the main food of such predators as weasels, martens, polecats, foxes, hawks and above all owls, which are so super-efficiently equipped to capture prey in a forest environment that they seem over-specialized. In the first place a night-hunting owl's broad wing surface, together with its velvet-soft primary feathers which are finely edged with flexible filaments that reduce air turbulence, enable it to fly silently. Secondly, although its frontally situated eyes command a total visual field of only 110°, this includes a 70°-field of binocular vision, from which its brain forms the 3-dimensional image essential to judging distance; and as John Sparks and Tony Soper have pointed out in their book *Owls*, they bob and pivot on their perches in order to obtain a variety of viewpoints and also to observe the relative movement of objects within their visual field as their heads turn. Morever, some species, such as shorteared owls and barn owls which habitually or intermittently hunt by day, can rotate their heads through 270° without moving their bodies. Again, although owls can perceive objects in virtual darkness—in light a hundred times less bright than that required by the human eye—the eyes of many species must also be equally efficient in broad daylight; for those that inhabit northern forests have to contend during the summer months with twenty-four hours of daylight. Finally, it would appear that nocturnally hunting owls do not actually require to see their prey, because they also have exceptionally acute hearing. This is not associated with their characteristic ear-tufts, which in fact register various emotions during display; but concealed behind the edges of their no less characteristic facial disks are greatly developed ear openings, and these external ears are attuned to such high-pitched sounds as the thin squeaks of rodents and the patter of their tiny feet over the dead leaves of the forest floor. To these small sounds an owl can orientate on a flight trajectory accurate to within 1° in conditions of absolute darkness. Such an accumulation of special hunting aids suggests that owls have problems, not apparent to us, in obtaining sufficient prey, particularly no doubt during the winter.

Northern hedgehogs also hibernate, normally when the thermometer falls to about 36 degrees F, but do so much less regularly than dormice, often continuing to hunt for food until the end of the year, and "sleeping" for no more than three months beneath heaps of leaves and brush or in hollows under the roots of old trees; but since they lack the hibernating dormouse's ability to raise heat production automatically they must wake up in very cold weather, if they are not to freeze to death, when no doubt they experience similar difficulties in obtaining food. Partial hibernation is the most usual method of surviving the food scarcity and low temperatures of winter. The chipmunk, having hoarded substantial supplies of dried fruits, seeds and mushrooms in underground chambers, constructs a soft bed of plant fibers on top of one store of food and curls up on this to sleep; but at intervals during the winter it wakes up to rid itself of wastes in another chamber and have a meal, before returning to sleep again. Likewise, ground squirrels in the Siberian forests store spruce and pine seeds in their burrows. Because they do not accumulate sufficient reserves of fat in the autumn they wake early at the end of the winter, but remain in their burrows, feeding on their stores. Even those unique members of the canine family, the raccoon-dogs which live in wet Asian deciduous forests, go into partial hibernation in the colder mountainous parts of their range, though some remain active throughout the winter in temperatures as low as minus 10 degrees F, and none become completely torpid, emerging occasionally from their hollow trees or rock caverns, especially during warm weather, to prey on a variety of small animals and insects, but especially on fish and amphibians on which they pounce in shallow waters.

The extent of hibernation also varies widely among bears, according to climate, locality, the availability of food and individual condition; but pregnant she-bears must hibernate or shelter in dens for periods of weeks or months during the winter because of the embryonic conditions of their cubs which are blind and hairless and no larger than guinea-pigs at birth. The further north a bear lives the greater the difficulty it will have in obtaining sufficient food during the winter, but it can avoid starvation by hibernating for variable periods, subsisting on some of the 3 or 4 inches of fat it has amassed during a period of intensive feeding in the autumn; whereas those inhabitating more southerly regions, such as the brown bears of the Carpathians, may not go into hibernation at all if the harvest of beechmast has been extra good. North American black bears, on the other hand, hibernate for most of the winter in hollow logs or rock caverns—steam-heated by hot springs in the Yellowstone National Park—or merely in shallow depressions lined with a few sticks, and no more than 3 feet in diameter. In such exposed "dens," very similar to those of European brown bears, the occupant curls up or lies on its side with nose buried in paws and allows itself to be snowed over. By contrast some black bears in Manchuria den up in the large poplar and lime trees that are a feature of the deciduous forests of that region. Two or three bears may occupy several "flats" high up in one giant poplar 80 or 100 feet tall, and when the trunk becomes plastered with frozen snow, gnaw air-holes above their flats. Bears are fully protected against extremes of cold by dense undercoats beneath their outer guard-hair, and it is heavy snowfalls blanketing their vegetable food, not low temperatures, that determine the dates on which they go into hibernation. Yet the habit of denning up persists among some races of bears living in regions where it would appear to be totally unnecessary. The rather large black bears of Florida, for example, habitually den up from early January until mid-March, despite the fact that their favorite palmetto berries are available throughout the normally warm winters.

The majority of bears are forest dwellers in greater or lesser degree because, although omnivorous, they are predominantly vegetarian, consuming enormous quantities of berries, fruits, nuts and grasses. Himalayan black bears, though standing 6½ feet and weighing 420 pounds, obtain much of their food in the trees, venturing out at dusk from their lairs in hollow trees or dry caves to raid orchards for apples and pears, apricots, peaches, mulberries and walnuts; but brown bears seldom climb trees once they are full-grown, when they may reach a stature of 8 feet and weigh upwards of 980 pounds. Although brown bears are now most numerous in the vast coniferous forests of the Siberian taiga, particularly in those parts where the forest is interspersed with marshes or where new vegetation is springing up from burnt areas, the more open country of birch-wood steppe provides them with better feeding; and in western Europe, where the few that remain have been driven into re-

Black bear cub

mote mountainous areas, they prefer mixed woods of conifers, beech and birch, which are associated with a luscious vegetation in the ravines or on the alpine meadows above. Such habitats supply them not only with beechmast, hazel nuts and berries— the favorite food of all bears—but with voles, ants and insects, and with grass on which they graze like cattle in the early summer as the melting snows recede, or plough up great tracts of hillside when grubbing for roots and tubers.

But although bears are primarily vegetarians, plants and fruits are only available in most parts of their range for five or six months out of the twelve, and for the remainder of the year they are omnivorous. In addition to acorns and beechmast, the buds and leaves of maples, aspens and mountain ashes, ripening maize and the pungent roots of the Indian turnip, American black bears rob squirrels of their hoards of nuts, as Manchurian black bears rob chipmunks, and lap up ants by the thousand as they swarm out of their shattered hills and galleries. They are as heedless of the ants' acetic acid as they are of the vicious stings of hornets, wasps and bees whose nests they plunder for their honeycomb. Frogs and toads, birds and their eggs, mice, chipmunks, ground squirrels and marmots, an occasional porcupine or trout or salmon—all are acceptable to black bears.

Despite their immense strength, forest bears are not physically equipped to prey on large mammals. The flattened, blunt-edged cheek-teeth of black bears are, for example, adapted to masticating tough, fibrous foods such as roots, grass and nuts. Nevertheless American black bears not only prey extensively on rodents, but also kill young deer and antelope and moose calves when they can catch them; and in the days when beaver were numerous, a black bear would stalk from one lodge to the next, intent on pouncing on one engaged in tree felling or dam building. Similarly, when European brown bears emerge from hibernation in the spring there is little food for them except frozen berries preserved under the snow, or ants, or perhaps the carcase of a reindeer; and at this hungry season a few individuals attack the young of wild boar, roe or moose, and occasionally adult moose and reindeer.

6: Introducing the Rain-Forest

There are three main regions of tropical rain-forest, located between 4° North and South of the equator. The most extensive covers a huge area of South America from southern Mexico to southern Brazil. The second is in south-east Asia and extends from south-west India and Ceylon to Malaysia and Indonesia; there is also rain-forest in north-east Australia, New Guinea and on some of the Pacific islands. The third and least extensive stretches for 1,000 miles uninterrupted from the west coast of Africa almost to the lakes of East Africa. True rain-forest is also found outside the tropics, in such regions as the Pacific coast of America, where warm rains and sea mists prevail from British Columbia to 60° N in the Yukon. Its constituents are, however, very different to those of the tropical rain-forest, since they comprise an upper canopy of such giant conifers as Douglas fir, sitka spruce, red cedar and hemlock, a middle layer of smaller conifers together with some broad-leaved deciduous trees, and an under-storey of bushes and ferns.

Tropical rain-forest can thrive in a hot climate with an annual rainfall of not less than 50 to 80 inches, providing that at least 2 inches fall in every month of the dry season, which must not normally exceed three months in duration. In these ideal conditions a vertical stratification is achieved, mounting from a ground vegetation of seedlings and herbs a couple of feet high; through a layer of dwarf trees, palms and shrubs from 6 to 15 feet in height, and a middle-storey of medium sized trees whose long spiring crowns, reaching upwards in search of light, do not form a continuous canopy; to an almost solid canopy formed by the crowns of tall trees averaging 120 feet in height, but broken here and there by the emergent crowns of giants 200 feet above the forest floor.

Although this analysis of the rain-forest's structure is broadly correct, and useful to the botanist and zoologist, since the canopy forms in the main a "tightly set mosaic, with each tree shaped to fit whatever space is available after its quiet, biochemical pushing and shoving with neighbours has been impressed upon its system of growth" (as Archie Carr has expressed it), it is in fact an over-simplification because in every storey there are shrubs and lesser and greater trees breaking up the pattern.

The development of this tiered structure is controlled primarily by the amount of sunlight that filters through from storey to storey, and the forest's power-plant (Carr's term) is housed in its green roof, for this, being exposed to full sunlight, is the zone of almost all photosynthetic activity; and since it excludes most of the wind, it is also responsible for much of the greenhouse-like tranquility of the rain-forest atmosphere and the stillness of the forest floor. In the deep humid interior of the forest the low growth has only two methods of reaching the sunlit zone of photosynthesis. If it is a potential tree it must shoot upwards, smooth and branchless, for 100 or 200 feet until it can thrust its leafy tip through the upper canopy, whereas the climbers, creepers and lianas are obliged to coil cable-like stems upwards around the trunks of the giants, while swinging out in looped festoons from the branches or dropping aerial roots.

Carr has said that an acre of rain-forest is one of the most dynamic acres on Earth, with the richest growth and the most advanced and intricate organization. The forest can also be regarded as a single composite community, none of whose plants and trees, invertebrates, reptiles, birds and mammals can exist independently of the others. With temperatures uniformly high throughout the year, the moist tropics provide the most favorable environment for terrestrial life and include the richest variety of animal life from invertebrates, especially ants and termites, to the largest predators; while "cold-blooded" reptiles and amphibians find conditions ideal in the tropical forest, for its equable temperatures, varying little from day to day beneath the canopy's insulating blanket, pose no problems of excessive heat or cold.

Since the evenly distributed monthly rainfall ensures that the forest never becomes too dry, there are always some trees and plants in leaf or flower or producing fruit at all seasons of the year. Its inhabitants can therefore specialize in particular foods or rely on a succession of crops, while the different layers of vegetation provide them with a generous variety of habitat niches. But to take full advantage of the fruits of the forest the majority of its inhabitants must be able to climb or fly or glide. Monkeys, apes and lemurs, rodents (mainly squirrels) and birds are therefore the characteristic tree fauna, though many of the reptiles are highly specialized for arboreal life. Snakes with long thin bodies have angled scales on their undersides enabling them to obtain a purchase on the bark of trees when climbing, while the feet of geckos and tree-frogs have hairy pads or suckers. Some snakes, lizards and frogs are "winged" and can escape predators by gliding or parachuting from one tree to another or to the ground. The paradise tree-snake, which both swims and climbs well, can, for example, contract its belly into a concave surface that traps air beneath it and serves as a parachute when it straightens its body sharply on launching into space, to make a controlled fall at a steep angle; and a tree-frog's very large webbed feet are not for swimming but to arrest its fall when it drops to the ground after a glide of as much as 45 feet. Tree-frogs actually spawn in the water-filled funnels of bromeliaceous plants or in nests constructed of leaves glued together with sterile egg-jelly. When the first tadpole hatches, the nest collapses into the water beneath, possibly as a result of some chemical action triggered off by the tadpole.

Fruit-eating mammals are particularly characteristic of the tropical forest, and are most vulnerable to its destruction. These can either climb up into its canopy like squirrels, or fly down into it like flying-squirrels, or colugos, or fruit-bats such as the flying-foxes, with their 5-foot wing-span, which are mainly restricted to the forest because they are dependent on a constant ripening succession of fruits, especially figs, from which they extract the juices, spitting out the pulp. Flying-squirrels, which have a worldwide range north of the equator and, unlike other squirrels, are nocturnal, sleeping by day in hollow trees or woodpeckers' holes or stick nests, can glide from tree to tree in flights of as much as 150 feet, or twice that distance over a downward slope, on the large skin flaps that stretch from the sides of the body to the feet. Victor Cahalane has described how a flying-squirrel, weighing only from 3 to 5 ounces, can control the angle, speed and course of its glide by varying the slack in one or both "wings":

> Mostly, however, it steers with its tail. In the take-off jump the tail is brought down with a jerk until it is straight out. Throughout the glide legs and tail vibrate with tension, ready to twist, raise or lower as circumstances demand. This may mean a sudden turn of nearly ninety degrees or more. Many

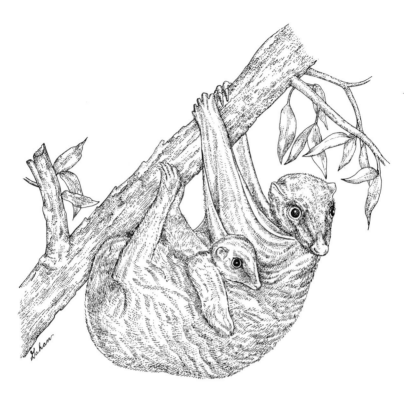

Colugo or flying lemur

lesser twists are required to avoid twigs and trunks of trees.
. . . Just as the little animal seems about to crash into the
ground at full speed, it flips its tail upward. Apparently the
hind feet strike first and absorb much of the shock.

But flying-squirrels cannot normally glide upward. They are
therefore as helpless as a bird with a broken wing if forced down
to the ground by a predator. Given time, however, an African
scaly-tailed squirrel can climb laboriously up a tree with the aid

of a series of horny, sharp-edged transverse scales beneath the base of the tail. These scales dig into the bark when the squirrel is clinging to the trunk, and by means of these and its claws it can lever itself upwards in the manner of a looper caterpillar.

The most efficient of all the mammalian gliders are the cat-sized greenish-gray colugos—the misnamed "flying lemurs" of Malaya, Indonesia, Indo-China and the Philippines. Except for the ends of their digits, their limbs are completely enclosed within a patagium of voluminous fur-covered folds of membrane which, when stretched taut in the gliding position, extends from the chin out to the hands, down to the toes, and back to the tip of the short tail. With the aid of its patagium, a colugo can glide more than 200 feet from tree to tree without losing more than 40 feet in height, to escape from a predator or when hunting in the twilight for insects and buds, flowers or fruit, from which it strains the juices through its comb-like lower front teeth; and when the young one is traveling with the female it clings to her belly fur within the patagium. Although a colugo spends most of the daylight hours slung beneath a branch or clinging to the trunk, it can also climb well with the assistance of its sharp curved claws, and is not impeded by the patagium which hangs loosely along the sides of its body.

Another characteristic feature of all rain-forests is that the various species of birds tend to live almost exclusively in their own particular storey. The Belgian ornithologist, James Chapin, for example, distinguished three distinct bird communities in the Congo's Ituri Forest: one community living near or on the ground; a second at mid-tree level; and the third community in the tree-top canopy. Carr has stressed the ecological importance of the canopy where, "by moving upwards or downwards only slightly as it travels, any animal able to grasp twigs can walk across the forest indefinitely and claim a home range or terri-

Monkey-eating eagle

tory." Such large fruit-eating birds as parrots, plantain-eaters, brilliantly plumaged touracos and hornbills exploit this niche. But though crested swifts may hawk for diptera high above the canopy, and crowned or monkey-eating eagles may soar above it, intermittently stooping to seize an unwary monkey or pa. ot from a branch, the great mass of birds inhabit the various storeys between the canopy and the ground, feeding on insects, nectar and soft fruit. And when they hunt through the forest in "armies"—another feature of tropical forest life—individuals from as many as forty different species of small birds, often accompanied by squirrels, may be included in a single army, with each species tending to keep to its particular storey when feeding on the insects flushed out by their mass movement or by the still greater disturbance associated with the hunting safaris of army ants. So too, hornbills follow monkeys to their fruit trees, plucking the small fruits delicately with the tips of their huge beaks and then throwing back their heads and tossing the fruit down their throats.

7: The American Rain-Jungle

In conjuring up a mental image of tropical rain-forest one thinks of Equatorial Africa, Malaya or New Guinea, but especially perhaps of Central and South America where its peculiarly primeval and hostile environment is most overwhelming. Emil Egli, who was a member of an expedition to the Amazon some fifteen years ago, has expressed this hostility:

Their vast swamps and morasses exhaling the sickeningly sweet, musky or putrid stinks of orchids and moon-flowers; their soaking humidity; their suffocating growth of trees and massed vines, lianas and parasitic creepers, inhibiting all sunlight except for rare shafts slanting between the giant columns of the trees. . . . There is no frost. No dryness. Flowers and fruit hang side by side in the eternal present of the always green foliage. All climatic enemies of plant life are here excluded. . . . Nowhere are birth and death so continuous and incessant. Hesitantly, as it were their funeral dance, the leaves fall from the trees to add to the rotting floor. The sap rises—there must be unimaginable streams of sap—from the roots to nourish this forest ocean, to extend its sway and to intertwine together. From earth to life, from life to mould, from mould to earth and from earth again to life, the cycle of nature is so vast that it baffles the mind.

And nowhere in all Earth's rain-forests are there such plagues of insects to render life a festering misery for man and beast as in the Americas—biting, stinging, poisoning black-flies, sand-flies, piumes and tabanos, sweat-bees, wasps whose stings can disable a man, as can those of the fire-ants. Ants and termites are everywhere, for most of the world's several thousand species of ants inhabit Amazonia, and their incessant attacks on all vegetable and animal life render certain regions virtually uninhabitable— as do those of mosquitoes, more than 140 species of which have been collected within a 5-mile radius of a field laboratory in Colombia.

> In many ways it is a forest of death [wrote Anthony Smith as recently as 1971 of the Mato Grosso]. There are great dead trunks, either lying flat or leaning on the living, or even standing vertically and surprisingly on their own. . . . Some tall trees, obviously flourishing at the top, are supported by half-rotten trunks, either soft and dusty on the outside or having a tough shell round a cavernous interior. One longs to find a whole tree, a tree whose bark is as pristine as a Norway spruce, whose leaves are uneaten, whose interior is entire. Even to find a whole leaf is a problem; the insects see to that.

Foremost in the defoliation of the South American jungle's vegetation are the *Atta* leaf-cutters or parasol ants, which are capable of entirely denuding a tree or shrub in twenty-four hours. They are of special interest to us because these ants of the New World are the only ones that practice the culture of fungi: a practice restricted elsewhere to the termites. The *Atta* exhibit a considerable range in size, and in any one nest the workers can usually be divided into maxima, media and minima. The maxima, armed with huge mandibles, perform the role of soldiers in defense against predators and never leave the nest; the media undertake the leaf-cutting; and the minima act as mini-soldiers. Riding near the top of a section of leaf being carried by a media worker and facing upward with wide-open jaws, the mini-soldier wards off the attacks of a small fly which circles above the worker while attempting to alight on it. If the fly succeeds in evading the mini-soldier and laying an egg in the back of the worker's neck, the latter is paralyzed for about a minute, but then slowly recovers and staggers back to the nest. However, if the egg subsequently hatches, the larva eats out the ant's brain.

The media workers cut out more or less circular pieces of leaf with their long scissor-like mandibles by pivoting around one leg, thus procuring disks proportionate to their size. The little green disks, the size of sixpences, are then carried back, held aloft like banners, along the roads that radiate from the colony's enormous underground nest, which is surmounted by a mound of excavated soil that may cover an area of as much as 50 square yards, and around which all the undergrowth has been stripped bare. There, according to John Sudd, the leaves are either first stored in large side-chambers where they may act as a tempera-ture control in those places on which the sun's heat strike most fiercely; or are scraped and licked by the carriers, perhaps to remove any foreign fungi that might infect the ants' fungi-cul-ture gardens, of which there may be as many as a hundred, each as large as a man's head. Then the carrier repeatedly cuts the leaf in half until it is left with a piece no bigger than its own head, while other workers take charge of the rejected halves. The small disk is now crimped round its edges by the ant's man-dibles, and both its surfaces are scarified until it is limp enough to be rolled into a ball and transported to a garden. There it is jabbed into a bed with a sharp movement of the ant's head, and firmed with its forelegs. The fungus thus cultivated in the gar-dens produces no spores, but at the tips of its hyphae small fruit-like bodies form, known as *gromatia*, on which the *Atta*'s larvae are fed. Since these *gromatia* cannot be produced artificially in the laboratory, they must be stimulated by some special treatment from the ants during cultivation. However, any new queen who survives the massacre of the mating flight by the hordes of predators attracted to it, and is successful in sealing herself into a hole in the soil, is able to introduce the fungus, since she transports a pellet of it in her infra-buccal pocket. When this fungus begins to grow she pulls out small tufts of it and—according to Sudd again—applies these to the tip of her abdomen where they absorb a yellowish liquid. She then replaces these tufts in the garden, and also lays a batch of eggs, some of which she deposits in the fungus, where they hatch. Other eggs, however, she breaks, both manuring the fungus with them and feeding them to the larvae that have hatched. Within three to five weeks of her mating flight the first workers have emerged from their pupae to take over the cultivation of the gardens and the feeding of the next batch of larvae.

Ants and the multitudes of other insects, together with the abundant blossoms and fruits of the rain-forest, provide food for a great variety of birds and arboreal mammals. Gorgeous quetzals—as magnificent as New Guinea's birds-of-paradise—feed high up in the trees of montane forests, flying to and fro from branches beneath the canopy to flutter in a vertical posture while picking off fruits or insects or small tree-frogs; toucans, macaws and parrots rely on the all-year-round bounty of fruits and seeds, cracking the nuts with their powerful beaks; and, above all, some 250 of the world's 320-odd species of humming-birds inhabit the Americas, a score or so exclusively in the rain-forest. Named for their vivacious beauty after every color and precious stone, and even for combinations of these as in the case of the ruby-topaz humming-bird, the minute air-filled platelets

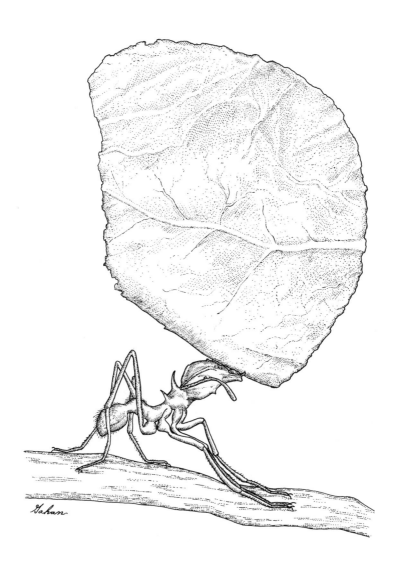

Atta *leaf-cutter (or parasol) ant*

on the surfaces of their feather barbules are responsible for an ir-
idescence that varies magically with reflecting light from second
to second.

Not only are they exquisitely beautiful, but they are also
marvelously adapted to their environment. To obtain nectar
from a diversity of vari-structured flowers, mainly red and especially the bromelias, they have developed specialized tongues.
These are so long that they can be hung out like pennants during courtship display—according to Walter Scheithauer who has
photographed their behavior intensively in his aviary—and their
pointed tips, divided like a snake's, are fringed with fine hairs,
directed inwards, which soak up the nectar and dispatch it into
the fine grooves that run backwards from the center of the tubular tongue. As an additional feeding aid their beaks have also developed into a variety of shapes and sizes, ranging from the tiny
probe of the thornbill to the vertically decurved beak of the
sicklebill and the rapier of the swordbill. Since the latter's beak
is 5 inches longer than its body, the bird is obliged to feed its
nestlings by injecting nectar through the coarse mesh of the nest
wall while hovering on whirring wings. But the use of these
precision intruments depends upon the humming-birds' mastery
of the most complex aerobatics, enabling them to hover, while
imbibing nectar, with wings rotating in the shoulder sockets at
rates ranging from 8 times a second in the largest Andean species weighing 20 grams, to 80 times a second or higher in a Bra-
zilian species weighing only 2 grams. The velocity of their wing-
speed is dramatically illustrated by Scheithauer's account of a
small Mexican humming-bird which, by the vibration of its
wings, almost forced a pane of glass, 15 feet by 6 feet, from its
frame in the front of his aviary: "The huge sheet of glass was
originally not very firmly anchored, and at a certain high
frequency of the wing-beats, the pane started to vibrate a little,

then increasingly strongly, until it vibrated so hard that the screws and angle-iron were torn away with such a loud crack that the plaster fell down from the ceiling."

In courtship flight the wing-beat rate may accelerate to a frequency of 200 times a second, a rate rather higher than that achieved by a bee—a mosquito's is 500—and Scheithauer goes on to describe how his Mexican humming-bird subsequently appeared to exploit the critical frequency at which its wing noise intimidated other species in the aviary, forcing a Brown Inca, which had previously often attacked it, to turn away when the critical "rattling" began.

A humming-bird hovering before its flower in a vertical posture can, according to the position of its shoulder joint, which alone is movable, remain stationary even in a high wind; and another of Scheithauer's captive birds, in order to penetrate the calyx of a hanging flower, approached the bloom from above and virtually became a flying drill, spinning rapidly on its own axis until it had bored a hole into the calyx. Yet, from this hovering position, a humming-bird can instantaneously fly forwards or backwards with equal facility; and the Swedish naturalist Jan Linblad, has pointed out that "the measurements of the requirements per hour and per unit of weight for a highly tuned helicopter are shown to be almost the same as those for a humming-bird." Nectar-sipping bats, which take the place of humming-birds when the latter are inactive at night, are also able to hover at flowers while their tongues, which are longer than their bodies, function like fuel pumps.

But this high wing-speed involves a humming-bird in a proportionately high output of energy, since the weight of its flight muscles may amount to more than a quarter of the body weight of a bird no larger, if its tail is excluded, than a bee. The bee humming-bird, for example, measures little more than 2 inches from beak to tail tip. Since this energy is expended very rapidly in the form of heat lost through its body surfaces, a humming-bird's daily food requirements may amount to seven or nine times its own weight, and it must feed almost continually throughout the hours of daylight on such high-energy foods as nectar, which is mainly fructose and glucose, while proteins are provided by large numbers of spiders and insects. Although it interrupts its feeding activities for an hour or so at midday, to sunbathe and sing, a humming-bird visits between 1,000 and 2,000 flowers of as many as 28 different species every day; intensifying its feeding rate towards dusk, prior to the inactive hours of darkness. In order to conserve energy during the night it can relapse into a state of partial or total torpidity, with respiration and heartbeat reduced and temperature lowered from the normal 104 degrees F to about 65 degrees F. In this state, when it becomes as stiff as a board and can be lifted from its perch, its metabolic rate is reduced to 1/15 of the normal: whereas a pygmy shrew, whose metabolic rate approaches that of a humming-bird, must feed night and day to stay alive. When the external temperature has dropped by 45 degrees F the bird can remain torpid throughout the fourteen hours of a winter night in the far north and south of its range, and in exceptional circumstances for two or three days at a time.

At forest edges and along the banks of rivers a heavy curtain several yards wide of interwoven vines and lianas, bromeliaceous plants and orchids falls to meet the bushes and climbing grasses of the ground-storey. The insects and fruits that thrive in this habitat exposed to the sunlight attract those mammalian inhabitants of the upper layers of the canopy, the monkeys. All the South American monkeys are predominantly arboreal, and a feature of their geographical distribution is that because there are so many immensely broad rivers and hardly less formidable tributaries, and because none of these monkeys can swim, a host of regional races have evolved. Most of our knowledge of their life-histories has been obtained on the island of Barro Colorado, which was originally a mountain top but was transformed into an island of 4,000 acres when the Chagres River was dammed during the engineering of the Panama Canal. Its rain-forest contains a rich fauna and flora, including some 58 species of mammals, 253 resident species of birds, 100 reptiles and amphibians and more than 20,000 insects; and in 1923 the island was scheduled as a zoological field base by the Smithsonian Institution. David Chivers has described in *Animals* how, at the beginning of the wet season, ominous clouds gather over the island in the afternoons, blotting out the sun and plunging the forest floor into darkness. Subsequently, drenching rains turn the forest trails into running streams and, as the months pass, there is less sun and more rain. But in the dry season:

Large blue butterflies flitted lazily among the trees catching the sunlight where it penetrated the canopy; stretched across the trails were the webs of exotic spiders; while on the forest floor itself there were frogs and toads, so cleverly camouflaged that they were scarcely distinguishable from the litter. . . . Above us the humming-birds whirred and flashed, toucans called harshly, and occasionally we caught glimpses of brightly coloured vine snakes . . . coatis and agoutis vanished into the undergrowth, peccaries crashed through the foliage.

Five species of monkeys co-exist within the restricted limits of Barro Colorado's rain-forest—red howlers, red spider monkeys, white-faced capuchins, night monkeys and marmosets; and it has been the fascinating work of a succession of zoologists to discover how so many different species and populations of monkeys—for each species includes numerous distinct clans—can compete peaceably for food and special territories. Chivers has summed up his own research and that of his predecessors in concluding that there is a tendency for each species to occupy its own particular ecological niche. Thus, while the howlers are exclusively arboreal in the upper layers of the canopy, the spider monkeys favor the middle layers, and the capuchins live mainly in the lower storeys, though frequently infiltrating higher layers and also descending to the forest floor. These three usually inhabit mature forest, whereas the marmosets probably prefer low scrub or the forest edge, as do the night monkeys which, being nocturnal, do not in any case compete with the other four, all primarily diurnal. No doubt also each species has a significant food preference. Howlers, for instance, have a special liking for figs, plums and cocoa beans, capuchins for palm fruits, and spider monkeys for the kernels of wild nutmeg and certain fattening bean-like nuts; and whereas the howlers feed intensively at each source of food, stripping a tree of its fruits, the capuchins pluck a fruit here and another there while moving as a troop on a broad front, crashing through the trees and calling to one another. And finally, a major factor in the maintenance of special territories by spider monkeys and especially by howlers is their employment of vocal displays.

The howlers have long made themselves conspicuous to explorers and naturalists by their voices, for the awesome serenades of the adult males at sunrise and sunset are estimated to be the loudest that any animal is capable of producing, and are comparable in volume to the jaguar's roar. "The first time I heard it, it seemed that all the jaguars on the Amazon were engaged in a death-struggle," wrote F. W. Up de Graff; and another explorer Leo E. Miller observed that, "At first there was a series of low, gruff roars that would have done credit to the most savage of lions, and the very air trembled. Then followed in quick succession a number of high-pitched, long-drawn wails or howls of tremulous quality that gradually died, ending with a few guttural barks."

William Beebe was also reminded of the jaguar when he heard this roaring of the red baboons, as the red howlers are known in Guyana:

> A red baboon raised his voice less than fifty yards away, and even the leaves seemed to tremble with the violence of the outburst of sound. A long, deep, rasping, vibrating roar, followed by a guttural inhalation hardly less powerful. After a dozen connected roars and inbreathings, the sound descended to a slow crescendo, almost died away and then broke with renewed force.

On another occasion Beebe wrote:

> A low, soft moaning came through the forest . . . It was deep, soothing, almost hypnotic. Then it gained in volume and depth until it became a roar, and from the heart of the bass there arose a terrible subdued trilling—a muffled raucous grating which touched some secret chord of long-past fear, when speech was yet unformed. The whole effect was most terrifying.

The red howler is the largest of the South American monkeys, weighing up to 30 pounds and standing almost 3 feet high, with a 2-foot-long prehensile tail. The adult's deep jaws contain a hollow chamber, the size of a lemon, in the throat, which serves as an amplifier; and as he contracts the muscles of his barrel-like chest and stomach, air is forced under pressure across an opening at the top of the sound-box, producing the characteristic roar. A. Starker Leopold has described how at first light the leader of a troop, an old male with a long silky beard, begins to warm up with a series of chesty roars:

> These gradually increase in frequency and volume until the sound is almost continuous. Then all the other members of

the band join in, and the sound is multiplied many times. The bedlam may last for several minutes; but finally the old male gradually unwinds with a series of shorter roars, and his troop follow suit. Echo dies among the trees and is lost in the silence of the rain-forest.

The howling of one clan is taken up by another clan in the vicinity and then by others until the majority of troops in the forest have serenaded; and on one occasion Chivers registered dawn choruses from as many as eleven groups in different parts of the Barro Colorado. But though this vocalizing is mainly conducted just before sunrise and again at sunset, any incident may trigger it off, and three troops will begin bellowing at each other in the middle of the night. A clap of thunder or sudden downpour or strong gust of wind, an aeroplane passing overhead, a flock of black vultures alighting in a troop's fig tree or even a passing flight of butterflies, a young howler falling out of a tree, or the approach of another clan or one of the large cats—any one of these occurrences is sufficient to set a troop roaring.

Although the volume of sound produced must proclaim a troop's whereabouts to every hunting jaguar within a range of two or three miles, it may serve as a communal defense against less powerful predators, for it has been known to scare away as large a cat as an ocelot from a juvenile it had already wounded. But apart from any personal satisfaction a troop of howlers experience from their serenading, its primary value is territorial. An average-sized troop contains more than 30 members, including perhaps 3 males and 7 or 8 breeding females, together with younger animals, though bachelor males tend to live on their own until old enough to take over the leadership of a troop. By howling, the various clans advertise the positions of their "roosting" trees and also their movements when they disperse to their fruit trees. As a general rule one clan goes out of its way to avoid close contact with another; but if two clans chance to approach to within a few hundred yards of each other, then they conduct a vocal "battle" that continues until one or other retreats from the frontier line, having avoided physical combat.

Chivers has summed up the howlers' territorial system in this passage:

> It seems that when a species is in the early stages of occupying a niche, the population spreads out in such a way that the contact between groups is reduced to a minimum, and when it does occur, the monkeys behave with tolerance, or only mild antagonism. . . . But the situation alters as the population density increases, and the amount of available food is thereby reduced. When this happens, the groups seem to adopt one of two alternative patterns of behaviour. Either they start to maintain and defend territories for their own exclusive use, or they adopt partially overlapping home ranges, within which the groups are still effectively separated by long-range spacing mechanisms. The basic difference is that the former is maintained by contact between groups, while the latter is maintained by avoidance.
>
> The population of howler monkeys on Barro Colorado is now twice what it was during the 1930's, and although the groups of monkeys are only slightly smaller than they were then, their ranges are only one-sixth as large. The chorus of howling (which starts at daybreak) certainly functions as a spacing-out mechanism, and the movements which subsequently occur throughout the day tend to increase the distance between the groups. Today there is as much as a 67 per cent increase between the home ranges of the howler monkeys, whereas before there was less than 10 per cent.

The red howlers are apparently liable on occasions to be as fatally fascinated by jaguars as the Indian langur monkeys are reported to be by tigers, and to be victimized in almost identically the same way. W. L. Schurz, for example, has described in

Brazil: The Infinite Country watching a jaguar standing at the foot of a tall tree and gazing fixedly up at a howler, which was crying piteously, while jumping from side to side at the top of the tree and peering down at the jaguar. Although the latter remained motionless, the howler, still crying, gradually descended lower and lower from branch to branch, and finally fell at the jaguar's feet.

Jaguars are, in fact, active predators in the trees, climbing branchless boles with surprising agility; and among their arboreal prey are the sloths. The warm, humid rain-forest provides an ideal environment for the peculiar two-toed and smaller three-toed sloths, which are unusual among mammals in not maintaining a constant body temperature: that of the two-toed varying, for example, from 75 to 91 degrees F. The various accounts of the behavior of sloths are so completely at odds that one despairs of discovering the truth about their habits in the wild state. The three-toed—generally stated to be a solitary animal, though as many as a dozen have been reported feeding in one tree—was believed to feed exclusively on the tender leaves and stems of *cecropias* or pumpwood which belong to the mulberry family, and to which the howler monkeys are also partial; to this item of diet, however, can probably be added leaves of the hog plum tree. The less specialized two-toed feeds on fruits, berries and the gourds of various vines, all with a strong acrid flavor. Holding a leaf by the stem the sloth nibbles round and round it until only a small disk remains, while swinging backwards and forwards from the branch, purring contentedly. But sloths pass much of their time sleeping, while hanging upside down and preferably at the thin end of a branch, for like the howler monkeys they favor high, slender branches, perhaps because these cannot support predatory jaguars and other cats.

To pluck a sloth in this position from its vice-hold on a branch would present even a jaguar with a problem, for the gripping power of its immense hooked claws rivals that of the giant ant-eater, and harpy eagles, swooping down into the canopy through the branches, are the main danger to sloths, as they are to monkeys.

Since a sloth does not employ its formidable claws either defensively or offensively, it must rely on other measures for protection against predators. It emits no detectable odor, though it has a keen sense of smell; its hearing is acute; and its thick skin and two coats of fur are tough enough to deflect an Indian's arrow. The fur, incidentally, grows in the opposite direction to that of most mammals, shedding the rain when it is in its favor-ite position, hanging beneath a branch. A sloth in a tree is also virtually invisible—to the human eye at least—since its long shaggy hair resembles withered gray grass, with a mossy tinge imparted by the algae that grow in the grooves of the hair-shafts. Since large numbers of a small moth actually lay their eggs in the sloth's hair, it is reasonable to assume that its larvae feed on the algae! Nor does a sloth become conspicuous when it moves, for this it does with extreme slowness. While still hang-ing upside down, it first tentatively extends one forefoot as far as possible along the branch and digs in its claws; then it stretches the other forefoot to the same spot, and simultaneously drags along both hind feet. Konrad Guenther made an interest-ing observation of a sloth using its intelligence to climb from a palm into another tree. When it initially slung itself forward along a palm leaf this was pulled so far down by its weight that it was unable to reach the tree: "Quietly it went back and em-braced two palm leaves, but as these were not rigid enough it made another attempt with three leaves, which did support its weight, and having reached the end of the three leaves it was able to reach and grasp the nearest bough of the adjacent tree."

The slothfulness of a sloth has perhaps been exaggerated. The nineteenth-century explorer Paul Fountain has stated that, when alarmed or in pursuit of a mate, a sloth travels through the forest so swiftly that not even an Indian can keep up with it for any distance, since it never makes the mistake of passing to a part of one tree from which it cannot reach the next. Nevertheless sloths occasionally fall to the ground, probably when trying to reach leaves or fruit hanging from branches too slender to bear their weight, or when attempting to escape from snakes; but while some observers have described them as virtually helpless on the ground, taking several hours to cover a few yards, others have stated that they can move remarkably quickly.

In the South American jungle hoofed mammals are largely replaced by plant-eating rodents such as capybaras, agoutis and the pacas or labas, all of which reach relatively enormous sizes. Capybaras in particular, resembling barrel-like sheep with dark-brown coats, short legs and massive log-shaped heads, reach weights of 112 or 126 pounds. A species of aquatic guinea-pig, the capybaras could be described as the hippos of South America, for during the day they wallow in groups of 3 or 4, or exceptionally as many as 50 or 60, among the huge Victoria lilies or other lake and riverside vegetation, frequently submerging for 8 or 10 minutes at a time; while at night they come ashore to graze, following well-trodden trails round the ponds and the winding canal-like ditches or bayous in the swamps, where jaguars hunt them. Stalking or lying in wait for deer or tapir or peccaries must often involve jaguars in hours of abortive hunting, and capybaras, and no doubt the other giant rodents, are their main prey, together with such small game as rats, mice, lizards and snakes, and such birds as turkeys, quail and tinamou, for, according to Indians, a jaguar can attract any bird or beast by mimicking its call. No doubt jaguars also kill many young tapirs, which are born during the summer months and remain with their mothers until they are a year or so old. Though three races of tapirs are widely distributed in the densest rain-forest, it is exceptional to encounter more than a pair together. Nocturnal, they lie up in the forest by day or wallow among the rushes at the forest edge to cool themselves and also to plaster themselves with mud packs against the incessant attacks of insects. In the cool of the evening they venture out to feed on fruits and leaves and the fleshy pacu-grass (*Podostemonacae*) which grows in luxuriant clumps on the rocks of rapids. Despite its great weight of 700 pounds a tapir travels noiselessly and rapidly through the densest jungle, but it has no physical powers of defense against large carnivores, though it may attempt to bite and stamp on a man: "His little red-rimmed pig-like eyes gleamed viciously, his proboscis was drawn up and wrinkled, exposing the yellow ugly-looking teeth, and the ridge of stiff hair on his neck fairly bristling with anger," wrote Thomas P. Bigg-Wither of one encounter.

When hunted by a jaguar, a tapir's immediate reaction is to head for the nearest lake or river, in which it can remain submerged for several minutes and travel 200 yards or more under water, though there is no evidence as to whether the South American species can walk on the bottom as the Malayan tapir does. Even if a jaguar is able to surprise a tapir asleep in a thicket of bamboo or prickly thorn and spring on its back, it does not necessarily prove an easy victim, for the jaguar must strike to kill instantly. If it fails to do this, the tapir, plunging through the bush or jungle, bursting its way through by sheer bulk and strength in its headlong rush to the water, succeeds as often as not in brushing the jaguar off its back against trees and branches. Algot Lange gives an amusing account of one such instance when he was camping in the jungle and was awakened in the early hours of the morning by a terrific roaring:

> I heard the crashing of under-brush and trees close upon us. My first thought was of a hurricane. The noise grew louder and more terrifying. Suddenly . . . the roof of the *tambo* collapsed and fell upon us. At the same instant I felt some large body brush past me, but the object passed swiftly in the direction of the creek.
>
> Someone now thought of striking a light to discover the extent of the damage. The *tambo* was a wreck; the hammocks were one trampled mass. Jerome followed the "hurricane" to the creek. . . . It was a jaguar, which had sprung upon the back of a large tapir . . . feeding in the woods behind our *tambo*. The tapir started for the creek in the hope of knocking the jaguar off its back by rushing through the under-brush; not succeeding in this, its next hope was the water in the creek. It had chosen a straight course through our *tambo*.

Before the introduction by Europeans of horses and cattle to the Americas the jaguars' main large prey, in addition to tapirs and deer, must have been the peccaries, as wild pig were the tigers' in Asia; and their only predatory rivals were pumas, as leopards were those of tigers. Although pumas range right through the jaguars' habitat they are essentially predators of pampas and mountains, rather than of the forests. But both can be found in the same jungle and, according to Indians, fight to the death, with the agile puma the victor in most instances despite its weight disadvantage. Nevertheless, one must presume that normally, as in the case of the more closely associated tiger and leopard, jaguars and pumas do not compete significantly for prey and territory; for were this the case, one or other would have been drastically reduced in numbers or driven to the extremities of its range. Although their measurements and weights overlap, with those pumas in the south of their range much larger than those in the tropics where they compete most directly with jaguars, the latter are considerably more massive and, though actually rather smaller than tigers, present the same appearance of immense strength, with their great girth, heavy chests and powerfully muscled forelegs.

There are two species of peccaries: the small collared peccary or javelina, standing less than 2 feet at the shoulder and weighing only from 30 to 65 pounds; and the white-lipped peccary or huangana, twice the weight of the javelina. The latter prefers scrub-forest, the huangana dense jungle, and both, though relying for much of their food on fallen fruits, figs and palm nuts, are omnivorous, including in their diet roots and tubers, grubs,

White-lipped peccary

worms, snakes, small animals and young turtles. The herds of from twenty to a hundred huanganas pass through the jungle with a low, eerie, moaning and a threatening rattle of tusks that resembles the clicking of a thousand pairs of castanets, and according to Up de Graff, "The strong acrid odour of the herd hangs in the air and on shrubs and overhanging branches long after the animals have passed, and can be smelt a full mile away"; for both species possess a large oily gland, positioned on the mid-line of the back a few inches forward of the very short tail. When an individual is sexually excited or alarmed or angry the long hair on its back is erected, exposing the gland, which emits a musky odor; while when two friendly animals meet, they may face in opposite directions and, with sides touching, rub jowls and necks rhythmically over each other's scent glands. The heavy residue of musk on rocks and trees suggests that it may also serve identification purposes and perhaps demarcate the boundaries of a herd's territory which, in the case of a herd of a dozen or score of javelinas, may be no larger than 2 miles in diameter.

One would suppose that such a strong scent would attract every jaguar in the neighborhood. However, although the small javelinas may be more or less defenseless against jaguars, huanganas are as formidable as the wild boars of Asia, being insensately ferocious and deceptively agile. Nevertheless, according to Indians again, every large herd is accompanied at a discreet distance by a jaguar picking off the stragglers. Leaping down from ambush in a tree, the jaguar kills a solitary peccary or one at the end of a file; then leaps up into the tree again to wait until all the herd has moved on, before descending to eat at its leisure. Occasionally, however, a jaguar errs in selecting a tree in which it is not able to climb out of reach of the herd; and there are a number of records of jaguars being slashed and torn to pieces, and also eaten, by an infuriated herd of huanganas. Should a jaguar be rash enough to launch its attack on the main body of the herd, its chances of survival may be slight.

Jaguars are generally reported to be much more numerous in the Mato Grosso and particularly in the swamp-forest of the southern Pantanal than in the forests of Amazonia. The obvious reason for this disparity is that neither predator nor prey can live permanently in those thousands of square miles of the Amazon jungle that are flooded to a depth of 50 feet during the 5 or 6 months of the rainy season, when as much as 30 inches of rain may fall in 24 hours. However, there are in both Amazonia and the Mato Grosso extensive areas of woodland no denser than that of an English park, where game and jaguars are, or were, very numerous. The perennial flooding of Amazonia, together with the colossal subsidence of river banks and the forest itself, must control, seasonally or permanently, the distribution of all animal life; and immediately after the floods have receded there is a marked absence of fauna. Some jaguars, and also pumas, travel for many miles down the flooded rivers on the trunks of trees; but the majority migrate to higher ground and especially to islands. Nearly all jaguar trails lead to rivers; and it is islands, rivers, marsh and swamp that are the normal haunts of jaguars in country less subject to flooding, because these are also the haunts of their prey. Of all the cats the jaguar is most at home in the water, roaming at night across the marshes and swamps so typical of the Mato Grosso, and along the banks of bayous and ponds, or straight through them when in pursuit of swamp deer, and swimming with ease across the broadest river with the tip of erected tail bent above the surface: whereas pumas swim slowly and awkwardly.

Jaguars are also considerable fish eaters, as one might expect them to be in what is regionally almost a semi-aquatic environment. Splashing about in the shallows, they hunt those gigantic freshwater fish, the arapaima, which may exceed 9 feet in length and 420 pounds in weight, and are powerful enough to tear themselves free from a jaguar's talons and escape into deep water. However, when hunting for moderate-sized fish, a jaguar usually takes up position on a log or branch projecting over the water and scoops them out with a paw; and it has now been established by reputable observers that jaguars also attract fish by deliberately tapping on the water with their tails, simulating the impact and disturbance of falling fruits and berries, on which some species of fish are accustomed to feed. Turtles and their eggs on riverine sandbanks must form a considerable item in the diet of many jaguars. Although the turtles may weigh as much as 280 pounds, they are invariably turned over on their backs, and Alexander von Humboldt described 125 years ago how, "by placing one paw on top of the turtle and skilfully biting out a round hole along the line of the junction between the back and front shields, the jaguar then scoops out the flesh with his paw and cleans out the shell without breaking it."

8: The Termites'
Incredible Civilization

The actual floor of the rain-forest, whether in South America, Africa or Asia, does not have an extensive vertebrate fauna. Although it may be dappled with sun-flecks when the sun is shining into the canopy, insufficient light filters through the dense upper layers of foliage to facilitate photosynthesis, with the result that there is little green vegetation, and the leaves of many shrubs and herbs, utilizing the duller end of the light spectrum, are deep purple or red. But under the floor is a world of teeming and furious activity. The fall of organic matter—dead leaves and flowers, fruit-cases, twigs and rotten branches, animal detritus—which is seasonal in the drier types of tropical forest characteristic of much of India, is constant and heavy throughout the year in the rain-forest. And if, to quote Carr again, "There was not an army of efficient small scavengers living in the soil to convert this rain of dead material back into living tissue, the whole community would grind to a halt, because gradually the pile-up would be so great that there would be nothing left for the larger forms, either animals or plants, to exploit. That is why the hosts of insects, tiny arthropods, and even tinier bacteria that live in the soil, are so important; they are the 'decay' agents, the reprocessors which break down the dead organic tissue into its chemical constituents and, in one way or another, turn it back into protoplasm again."

Bacteria, protozoa, algae, fungi, termites, true ants, millipedes, centipedes and earthworms all toil unceasingly. Although the latter are less numerous than in temperate regions, they are nevertheless important soil cultivators, and are often of gigantic size and reputed to defend themselves from the attacks of birds by squirting coelomic fluid through their dorsal pores to a height of 10 or 12 inches. So effective is the work of the reprocessors, and in particular that of the ants and termites because of their habit of transporting vegetable food underground, that there is far less debris in the rain-forest than in temperate forests. Indeed, since a single termite—out of the million millions—is capable of consuming about 2 cubic centimeters of dead vegetation annually, little of the latter is left above ground to rot down, and much of the forest floor is only thinly carpeted with leaves, or even bare of covering.

If the rain-forest is to be ecologically viable there must be a relatively rapid breakdown and processing of its woody constituents, in which is locked up the wealth of nutrients taken from the soil. These must be returned if the soil is to retain its fertility. The essential agents in this vital reprocessing of the dead wood are the termites, the most prevalent of rain-forest insects around the globe. Although they do not usually attack living wood, they take advantage of wood partly broken down by fungi and, forcing an entry through a dead root or branch, begin eating out the heart of a tree that has not yet reached maturity. Since there may be a thousand termitaries in a single acre of forest, each inhabited by tens of thousands of termites or as many as 10 million, and since 1 million termites are capable of consuming 12 tons of wood annually—the equivalent of a large tree together with its roots and branches—their overall influence on the forest's economy is patent. Yet termites, unaided, are as incapable as man of digesting cellulose.

There are two major groups of wood-eating termites. One group processes the cellulose with the aid of a multitude of protozoans, which inhabit a termite's gut or hind intestine in such numbers that they may constitute almost one-third of the insect's total weight; the other group cultivates extensive subterranean gardens within the termitary on prepared beds of chewed wood and leaves mixed with excreta on which spores of a certain fungus are sown. Bacterial fermentation in the gardens generates a constant temperature around 86 degrees F, and humidity within the termitary is maintained at near saturation point, while the circulation of this moist warm air is engineered by the 5 degrees difference in the temperature prevailing in the upper and lower parts of the termitary; though some species construct vertical air-ducts in the outer ridges of their termitaries, and these are blocked or opened as required to maintain a constant temperature in the queen's chamber near the bottom. Such conditions are ideal for the optimum growth of the fungi, enabling the developing hyphae to break down the cellulose and produce fructifications in the form of minute spherical nodules which, according to some authorities, are the termites' main food, though others believe that they are of little importance as food, but increase the life-span of the workers by providing them with essential enzymes.

A termitary has been described as the most specialized, most intricately organized, and most efficient civilization of the animal world. Indeed, the South African naturalist Eugène Marais considered it to be the most intelligent, most logical and best adapted to the problems of existence on Earth of any that has yet evolved, superior to those of the true ants, of bees and even of man himself. So it ought to be, for in comparison with *homo sapiens'* relatively brief experience of these problems and the seventy-million-odd years' experience of ants, bees and wasps, termites have had about two hundred million years in which to develop their society. But it is a society that flourishes only under communal conditions. No solitary species of termite is known. Yet, it is difficult to conceive of any creatures worse adapted, superficially, to existence on Earth than termites. Blind and soft-skinned, they are intolerant of changes in temperature or humidity, or of exposure to sunlight and, with certain exceptions such as the harvester termites, rarely voluntarily venture out of the termitary once the queen has founded her community. Nevertheless, by entombing themselves in a hard-shelled fortress, they survive floods and the incessant attacks of ants and a host of other predators, while in order to gain safe access to the trees and logs that provide them with food and building materials, they construct elaborate covered runways or tunnels that may extend 100 yards from the termitary. It is a problem to determine how they discover these external sources of food, though the construction of the subterranean runways is perhaps preceded by surface surveying by soldiers, since these have been found above ground at night at some distance from the termitaries.

The majority of termitaries are subterranean or located within a log or even in branches in the forest canopy; though some are constructed in the form of pagodas with one cap above another or, when plastered on to the trunks of trees, in series of chevrons, for the purpose in either case of shedding the run-off from heavy rain. But we are particularly interested in those which, although their foundations are underground, are built upwards into mounds a few inches or several feet high, and can be opened for inspection. "Unseen, labouring endlessly in the centres of rotting trees, and under the carpet of fallen leaves, the termites chew away at the woody fabric of the forest" (wrote Carr), building up their relatively colossal edifices. Marais believed that they neither rested nor slept for the duration of their life-spans, but in termitaries of the black-mound species on the South African veld, groups of workers have been observed standing motionless with heads together for a few hours at a time in some of the cells. Be that as it may, more than one ton of soil can be excavated, particle by particle, in the space of six days by the ¹/₅-inch-long workers of a single termitary, and it has been calculated that those built by the small Australian *Eutermes* may contain 11,750 tons of microscopic sand grains, while a man-made building on the scale of the African *Bellicositermes* termitaries, 20 or 30 feet high and 45 feet in circumference at the base above ground, would reach the height of the Matterhorn (14,760 feet).

The tough outer skin of a termitary shields a honeycomb of cells and galleries. Its material is more resistant to weathering than any other, including rock and man-made plastic, for every particle of clay or sand is bound by a "cement," composed of the workers' saliva and liquid excreta, which sets hard within a few hours. Within his magnifying glass Marais observed that the workers rolled every grain of soil in their jaws, coating it with a sticky fluid (obtained from the fungus gardens) which evaporated very quickly, before placing it in position when repairing a breach in the outer skin; and he was puzzled by the problem of where the termites obtained the enormous masses of soil, and also the millions of gallons of water, involved in the construction of a large termitary over a period of years. Since there are no correspondingly large cavities within a termitary, he concluded that the soil was extracted from innumerable minute cracks and crevices. However, within a termitary there is a hollow space, partially or entirely filled with cells formed of fungal mold, and it is now known that more than half the cellulose digested by the termites, and subsequently further processed by the garden fungi, is in fact employed for building purposes.

From the subterranean foundations of the termitary the workers build upwards, partly to secure more efficient ventilation as the population increases, and partly to evade periodic floods which may destroy young colonies. The actual size of a termitary may be determined by the amount of food and water available in a particular locality. S. H. Skaife has pointed out that even on a warm day, with the air temperature around 86 degrees F, the members of a foraging band of termites require more than six hours to travel along their covered ways to and from a food source 100 yards from the termitary; while on a cold day, in a temperature of about 50 degrees F, such an expedition takes twenty hours or so. Therefore, after it reaches a certain size, a colony is confronted with the problem of obtaining sufficient food within a tolerable distance of the termitary for its 10,000 or 50,000 or possibly several million inhabitants; and when this climax is reached after twenty or twenty-five years there is no further increase in the population, and no further enlargement of the termitary. For some years the status quo is maintained; but then the population begins to decrease and, after an existence of thirty years in some species or perhaps seventy-five years or longer in others, the colony finally dies out, leaving the empty shell of its termitary as its monument.

The first duty of the founders of a new colony of termites is to ensure a plentiful supply of water with which to create suitable conditions for rearing the first batch of workers and soldiers. When the temperature is rising between 11 A.M. and 4

P.M. on fine days, or at dusk when there are fewer predators about, but in either case after a heavy shower or after the rainy season has set in, streams of thousands of winged termites, twenty times larger than the workers, pour out of small exit-holes in the termitary. It is not clear why these variable conditions should stimulate this swarming, but the dominant urge of these potential queens and kings is to *fly*. Their flight may cover only a few inches, or extend for several miles, and thereby result in the dispersal of possible new colonies; but not until the princess—as she is more precisely termed at this stage—has made her flight and, on coming to earth, instantly discarded her wings from their hinged attachment to her body, does she raise the tip of her abdomen and send out a signal, presumably odoriferous, to any male searching for a female that has survived the attacks of the hosts of predators attracted to the swarming; hence the urgency of the queen to get rid of her encumbering wings. But there is no mating until the princess, with the prince following an inch or two behind her, has located a suitable place in which to excavate a hole; indeed it is possible that they do not mate until the following spring.

If they survive the winter in their small hole then, according to Marais, both termites work incessantly throughout the twenty-four hours in the spring, driving perpendicular passages down to moist soil. In hollows in these passages they prepare the first gardens, fertilizing them with finely chewed and partially digested dry wood, and irrigating them with drops of clear shining moisture that they stored in their bodies when excavating the damp soil. When the gardens are saturated a white fungal mold develops, possibly derived from pellets of mycelium transported in the queen's infra-buccal pockets from the original termitary. In these gardens the queen lays her first eggs, and subsequently feeds the resulting larvae with drops of the irrigating liquid. Marais goes on to describe how subsequently the queen and her consort are able by some means to retard the growth and development of the mycelium, and there is an extraordinary rise in the temperature of the gardens; while all the food that they, and later the new workers, have partially digested is dumped on the gardens, where it undergoes further treatment by the fungal mold: "The gardens are digestive organs without which the community could not exist even for one day." At a later stage small gardens are established in the depths of the termitary, and these are constantly watered by the workers, and serve as seed-beds of mycelium for new gardens.

Once the queen has reared workers to run the day-to-day affairs of her new colony she becomes its voluntary and sole reproductive organ, imprisoned in absolute darkness deep within the termitary in a cell, whose entrance (and exit) soon becomes too small for her to use, until after perhaps ten or fifteen years of prolific egg-laying she has become a gigantic and, to the human eye, obscene and pathetic, bloated monstrosity, more than 4 inches long and 2 or 3 inches in girth and many thousand times the size of the workers that attend her and the still active king who, curiously enough, remains with her. It has been claimed that she never stops laying throughout her life-span, producing perhaps 50,000 eggs every twenty-four hours. But this is almost certainly a gross exaggeration, though under laboratory conditions queens have laid more than 5,000 eggs per day; and it is more probable that their production is controlled by the amount of food available in the termitary, and that they in fact lay several hundred or thousand eggs over a period of a few days, and then rest.

Of the many problems posed by the marvelous civilization of the termitary the most perplexing is that of who or what controls the infinitely varied individual and corporate, daily and seasonal, activities of the tens of thousands or even millions of inhabitants. Marais was in no doubt that by some inexplicable power the queen was the sole controller, despite her total immobility and detachment from the majority of her subjects. This was not mere speculation on his part, for he observed that when he divided a termitary into two sections by the insertion of a metal plate of the thickest galvanized iron, and then killed the queen, all directed activity by the workers ceased in *both* sections. No one, so far as I am aware, has offered any explanation of this particular experiment; but its implications are not appli-

Termite queen with workers in nest

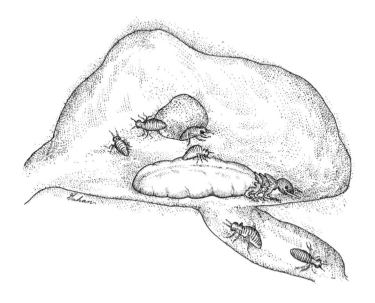

cable to all species of termites. The black-mound workers, for example, prevent some princesses and princes from flying away during the swarming, and hold them in reserve against the death of the brood queen. Skaife has suggested that the multifarious activities of the community are in fact controlled by the workers, with each different activity being initiated by specialized older workers, whose lead the others follow. This is a plausible suggestion so far as it goes, for it is the workers that dispose of the queen, when she is no longer able to fulfil her egg-laying function, by literally sucking her to death until only her empty husk remains; and it is workers that regulate the numbers of soldiers which, since they have to be fed by them, are a drain on a community's resources, restricting their strength to the minimum necessary for the adequate defense of the termitary—about 5 per cent of its total population.

Despite the protective walls of their cemented fortresses, termites are preyed on by multitudes of carnivorous ants—their immemorial persecutors—by spiders, wasps and beetles, by many species of birds, by lizards, burrowing snakes and even, on forested mountain slopes, by burrowing tree-frogs which never visit water, and by such mammals as golden moles, long-nosed elephant shrews, possums, pangolins, aardvarks and aard-wolves, and various kinds of ant-eaters and bears. When the virgin princesses and princes swarm out of the termitaries for their nuptial flight, they go forth wholly unprotected, though they are sometimes escorted to the exit holes by workers and soldiers, and perish almost to the last insect under the attacks of the hosts of predators attracted by their swarming. Their decimation illustrates what used to be known as the "balance of Nature." On the one hand the continued existence of termites depends upon an essential minimum of princesses and princes surviving the holocaust; on the other hand, if too many survived to found new colonies, then the competition between these might result in one exterminating the other or, alternatively, their inroads upon the wood resources of the forests might become so overwhelming as to result in the same catastrophe. As it is, there may be as many as nine different species of termites occupying one termitary, each with its own walled-off quarters and external foraging galleries; and there can be internecine warfare within the termitary. Scores of "guests," or inquilines, from mites and spring-tails to the larvae of flies and beetles, also live in the termitaries, and at night they may be lit with the lamps of hundreds of small glow-worms emerging from their holes.

Only pangolins, ant-eaters and bears are physically equipped to break open termitaries, though the black iguanas of New Guinea and the large monitor lizards of Africa and Asia are also reported to do so in order to lay their eggs within them, after tearing open a wall that has been softened by heavy rain; the termites then repair the breach, sealing the eggs in a predator-proof incubator. Carnivorous ants and certain groups of beetles are also able to force an entry, and although such breaches are immediately repaired by the workers, under the protection of the monstrous soldiers, the invaders may be in sufficient strength to exterminate the termites in one section while the remainder of the termitary is being sealed off. Some species of termites are reputed to evacuate their termitaries when invaded by army ants and, with a hardly credible reversal of normal behavior, march above ground to some distance from these, returning to them after the ants have moved on; but there may have been confusion here with the behavior of some harvester termites which, unlike other termites, obtain their vegetable food above ground, marching by night or on cloudy days in immense armies to collect plant debris or lichen from the trunks of trees. Most termites, however, defend their homes to the death, with the workers of some species actually rupturing one side of their bodies and exuding a sticky substance that ensnares attacking ants.

Most termitaries rely on a soldier caste for their defense. Some soldiers are armed with biting mandibles almost as formidable as those of army ants; but since termites evolved chemical warfare long before man had even been contemplated by Nature, they have had time to improve on the primitive military equipment of biting mandibles and to replace these by a tubular snout: a long horn-like needle or syringe that tapers from the opening of the frontal gland. The latter occupies almost the whole of the massive triangular head, which has no mouth and bears no trace of any sense organ except the two antennae. The tubular nozzle, or nasus, acts as a highly efficient repellent, capable of quickly producing an effective barrier of volatile odor that causes attacking ants to retreat. Other types of nasute soldiers are capable of squirting drops of sticky liquid containing a stinging acid to a distance of 2 centimeters and this fluid gums together the invading ants' jaws and legs, and possibly also affects their breathing, for Joy Adamson has described seeing a strange formation of pale-colored termites arranged defensively in several parallel formations around a hole. When a stream of army ants approached, the termites immediately stiffened and the majority of the ants, though twice their size, at once retreated: "The termites spat at the few stragglers who remained behind, ejecting a sticky substance which probably affected the respiratory organs of their victims, for after a few wriggles they died."

Harvester termites are always accompanied on their food-collecting sorties by nasute soldiers which, with nozzles elevated, run restlessly up and down the flanks of the long files of carrier workers and, on encountering ants or other predators, shoot fine white threads of repellent at them. Their curious habit of beating their heads in unison among the leaves of a forest path, and producing a rhythmic rustling resembling the slow regular footfalls of a stalking animal, is presumably associated with some form of communication.

9: Army Ants

The termites' chief enemies, the large black ponerine ants and the 200 species of army ants, are all members of a single sub-family, the Dorylinae. The African ponerine, *Megaponera foetans*, is related to the slightly larger, inch-long *Paraponera*—colloquially known as the 4-sting or 4-time ant because the stings of four ants are reputed to be lethal to a man, or as the 24-hour ant because its sting can paralyze a man for twenty-four hours. While the effects of their stings on a man may have been exaggerated, it is not disputed that they are excruciatingly pain-ful, cause the lymphatic glands to swell, and in many cases oblige the victim to lie up for a day or two with a fever. The stings of another relative, the 2-inch-long *Diponera*, the largest known ant, are less potent. The ponerines, living in colonies of only 100 to 400 in subterranean nests, and raiding singly or in dispersed columns by night, are among the more primitive ants, for their society virtually comprises only two castes—workers and males. Their queens closely resemble workers, while the small defenseless males rely for protection on workers with dis-proportionately large heads and formidably toothed mandibles. The *Megaponera*, migrating from one worked-out termite area to another, are perhaps even more deadly enemies of the termites, especially of the swarming princes and princesses, than are the army ants, for they employ both conventional and chemical weapons. A single penetration of the sword-like sting, which this ponerine achieves by seizing its victim with its jaws and thrusting forward its abdomen, paralyzes a termite instantly and is also fatal to small mammals, for it is associated with an injection of venom from its anal glands. This pungent and acrid liquid volatilizes quickly in warm air, and must prove lethal to termites within the confined space of the termitary.

In contrast to those of the ponerines, the colonies of army ants are hundreds of thousands or millions strong: numbering possibly 10 million in the case of the largest species of American *Eciton*, and possibly 15 or 20 million in that of the African *Anomma*. The latter are popularly known as driver, safari or siafu ants, and the details of their complex organization and raiding activities would fill several volumes, largely as a result of the researches of T. C. Schneirla and his team of assistants; so we must be content here with a general account.

The driver ants occupy temporary nests in holes in the ground or beneath fallen trees for periods ranging from a week to a couple of months, whereas the various species of *Eciton* fashion "bivouacs" of their own bodies for a single night only or for as long as three weeks. By clasping one another's legs with their sharp curved claws, tens of thousands of *Eciton* workers form a hanging cluster from a branch 150 feet up in a tree or from the side of a log on the ground, with their queen and larvae deep within and near the top of the cluster, where the temperature is maintained at a level a degree or two higher than that without. Galleries percolating through the living mass, as if through a conventional nest, permit the workers to carry out their normal duties of feeding and grooming the larvae and queen and other activities.

The raiding patterns of both driver ants and *Eciton* are, remarkably, geared to and incited by the rhythm of the reproductive cycle. In the nomadic phase, which is associated with the interval when the larvae are developing—a period of about three weeks in the case of the driver ants and from five to seven weeks in that of the *Eciton*—the workers are feverishly active. Stimulated by the thousands of squirming, wriggling larvae, they not only engage in massive group actions within the "nest," but stage very large massed raids for prey every day, with several marauding armies often deploying in different directions at one time. Some species of *Eciton*, however, cease all raiding at dusk or even at midday, when the marauders return to their previous night's bivouac; but instead of occupying this bivouac for a second night, its position is either shifted in the evening or, if raiding has ceased at midday, those ants that have not gone out with the raiders follow up along the line of one of the hunting columns, which may have covered a distance of 350 yards. Somewhere along this line there is a confrontation between the outgoing ants and those returning with booty from their raiding, traffic becomes congested, and in due course some ants begin to cluster and provide the incentive for the formation of the new bivouac, situated at a point suitable for opening up new raiding country the next day. The mind boggles at the logistical problems involved in transporting 250,000 larvae from one bivouac to another, settling them in the cluster, and supplying them with food from the booty brought back by the raiders! During this "migration" the queen runs about midway in the concourse, keeping workers close round her (or even carrying them) by the unique contact-odor she secretes; and this pervasive and attractive odor, and also that of the larvae, is an additional factor in establishing a focal point around which the bivouac is formed.

The same procedure is followed on succeeding days; but

when the larvae spin their cocoons, prior to pupating, the work-ers' activity diminishes and for a period of three weeks or so they return daily to the same bivouac from their raids. During the ultimate seven or ten days of this "rest" period the un-typically wingless queen lays the quarter of a million eggs that are barely sufficient to replace the losses among the workers, whose life-span is perhaps no more than a couple of months. The metamorphosis from pupae into adult ants occurs more or less simultaneously, and this sudden addition of tens of thou-sands of highly energetic young workers stimulates the older workers to a new frenzy of activity and precipitates another nomadic phase. The fact that colonies of army ants are in a per-petual state of reorganization must increase the restlessness of the workers, and this state of flux contrasts with the stability of most other ant colonies, typified by those of the tree ant, *Azteca*, which is so attached to its permanent nest that if its tree is felled the entire colony remains within the tree and dies with it.

The raiding phases of the driver ants are less rhythmical than those of the *Eciton*, because they "rest up" at more variable inter-vals and usually for longer periods, while the colony queen lays the prodigious number of perhaps 1½ million eggs. In the course of the year she may therefore possibly lay more eggs than does the termite queen. The raiding sorties of the driver ants are also more prolonged and extensive, continuing for from eight to ten hours, and at the conclusion of a raid more than 20 per cent of the participants are carrying booty back to the nest. Accord-ing to Sudd, when a sortie of driver ants is imminent, very ac-tive individuals stream out of the nest and scurry frantically about in all directions, and eventually the remainder of their colony deploys in dense columns along those routes most fa-vored by these pioneers. Advancing on a front of 15 yards at a rate of about 20 yards an hour, the immense army marches in orderly formation, flanked by walls of huge soldiers whose large heads are equipped with powerful scimitar-shaped mandibles, despite the fact that none of its members possesses even the most rudimentary eyes, for each ant picks up the attractive chemical deposited by the ant ahead, and contact within the swarm is maintained by a communal odor.

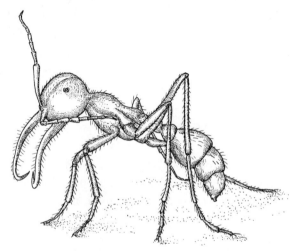

American Eciton, *or army ant, soldier*

It has often been observed that none of the other inhabitants of African forests evince any awareness that driver ants are raiding until the main army is within 20 or 30 yards of them, when their odor is detectable and antelope and pig become nervous; for they make no mechanical noise, unlike the *Megaponera* which, by rubbing one part of the body over ridges on another part, produce a shrill whistling that attracts other workers when one has met with some accident. In South America, however, if not in Africa, the raiding armies of *Eciton* are betrayed by the calls of ant-birds, when individuals of a dozen different species of these birds, all piping, whistling, twittering and churring, accompany a single army in order to feed on the insects and invertebrates the ants flush out. *Eciton* armies are also disclosed by the buzzing of certain parasitic flies that lay their eggs in the prey being transported by the workers, and by other flies which swoop down on any ant straying from the main columns in order to suck the juices from the prey or larvae it is carrying.

Driver ants raid most actively at night and on overcast days, especially at the beginning of the rainy season when they engineer surface tunnels cemented with saliva, though a considerable proportion of their prey is obtained underground at any time. During the most stimulating phase of larvae development they break their normally orderly raiding columns and fan out on a wide front, exploring every hollow log and swarming to the tops of the tallest trees; crossing the swiftest streams by forming living bridges or rafts of their own bodies, linked by entwined legs and mandibles, or utilizing telephone wires to traverse broad rivers; even extinguishing small fires through the medium of the soldiers, whose pyres of bodies enable the workers to swarm on. With few exceptions every creature, alive or dead, in the forest is attacked, whether grubs, insects, snakes, birds or mammals. Among the latter must be included even elephants, which are reputed to be driven demented by numbers of ants entering their tusks. Whether or not this is literally true, the game warden, Charles Pitman, has described an instance of a big bull twisting and turning on slippery ground in a series of figures-of-eight in desperate attempts to rid itself of its tormentors, before ultimately heading for the nearest water a mile distant.

The majority of the ants' victims are no doubt located randomly in the course of their intensive exploration, though they also appear to be attracted by ground vibrations, and it is generally stated that no animal that cannot leap or fly out of their way, or is not armed with a protective shell or effective chemical repellent, can survive their raids and that, in their passing, square "miles" of forest are denuded of life; but though raiding safaris are particularly efficient during the periods of their restless nomadic phases, they probably overlook 50 per cent of potential prey in the ordinary course of events. Nevertheless, they seem capable of intelligent application if confronted by an unusual type of prey. For example, only a small proportion of driver ants ever encounter snails, and W. B. Collins has described what happens when, on first attacking a snail, the ants are thwarted by its copious secretion of slime, which prevents them from obtaining a grip with their mandibles:

> So long as the snail can maintain a coating of mucus over its tender exposed body, it is safe. The ants solve the problem by foraging for crumbs of soil. These they collect one by one, piling them on to the mucus. The soil absorbs the mucus. In response the snail secretes more mucus. The ants bring more soil. They continue to collect soil and heap it on the mucus until the snail exhausts its supply.

There is, however, at least one forest inhabitant whose defenses the driver ants have not been able to master. This, not surprisingly, is another ant, the vegetarian tree or tailor ant, *Oecphylla*, which is in fact immune from the attacks of any predators. Tailor ants, unable to tunnel into wood, inhabit conical-shaped cocoon-like nests in the canopy, which they construct in the most ingenious manner by pulling leaves together. After from one to three hours of complicated maneuvering by two or more workers, two leaves touch and are then glued together by threads of a sticky fluid, which the workers obtain by gently squeezing their silk-producing larvae—oddly enough these do not spin cocoons—and this operation has been described by Sudd:

> A few large workers appear, each with a half-grown larva in its jaws. The larvae are held about one-third of the way back from their head end with their backs towards the worker's body. . . . The worker walks about the leaf edge with its larva until it finds a stretch free of ants. Then it touches the larva with its antennae. The larva thrusts out its head segments until it touches a leaf with them. As soon as it has touched one of the leaves the worker moves it across to the other leaf and so on, backwards and forwards from leaf to leaf, so that a zigzag of silk is laid between the leaves. The zigzag is so close set that adjacent threads of silk stick together to form a continuous sheet between the leaves.

Although the tailor ants are fierce and efficient fighters, tolerating no other insects in their trees, they do not actually attack driver ants; but the latter are apparently repelled by the sharp pungent odor of the acid they exude. This is so effective that even if a number of driver ants are thrown experimentally on top of a single tailor ant, they do not attack it, but scurry away.

Birds and such specialist ant-eaters as pangolins take some toll of army ants, more particularly of the smaller, relatively defenseless workers; and they suffer heavy casualties in battles with the numerous species of other ants and termites they attack, and from the chemical repellents of beetles and bugs. But floods and, in bush country, fires and droughts—they are extremely vulnerable to desiccation—must be the main factors controlling their huge populations, together with the rapid turnover of workers and the problems involved in obtaining sufficient food for the immense number of larvae and in transporting this to them.

10: In the African Rain-Forest

The African rain-forest covers two main regions. The smaller comprises Upper Guinea, and the larger the Congo Forest whose infinite canopy of great trees roofs in 600,000 square miles of Lower Guinea. The natural boundary between the rain-forest and the savanna grasslands is a fringe of shrubby vegetation and low trees. In places it may be only 10 yards wide, but the frequent bush fires that sear and blacken the plains usually peter out in it before reaching the forest. Thus a naturalist may find himself standing on a dividing line between the breast-high green grass and sunlit open woodlands of the savanna on his one hand, and on his other the deep dim shade of the rain-forest where the light, filtered through a million million leaves, has been variously compared to the greenish glow in an aquarium or to that of a European beech wood in its spring green.

Gerald Durrell has described the rain-forest of the Cameroons:

Tremendous trees, straddling on their huge buttress roots, each with its cloak of parasitic plants, ferns and mosses. Through this tangle the lianas threaded their way, from base to summit, in loops and coils and intricate convolutions. On

reaching the top they would drop to the forest floor as straight
as a plumb line. In places there were gaps where one of the
giant trees had been felled, or had fallen of its own accord,
and here the secondary growth ran riot over the carcase, and
everything was hung with the white and deep yellow flowers
of convolvulus, and another pink star-like flower in great profusion. In and out of these blooms flipped the sunbirds, glint-
ing metallically in the sun, hanging before the flowers for a
brief instant on blurred and trembling wings. On the dead
trees, bleached white as coral against the green, there were
groups of pygmy kingfishers, small as a wren, brilliant in
their azure blue, orange and buff plumage, with their crimson
beaks and feet. Flocks of hornbills . . . would fly wildly
across the road uttering loud maniacal honkings, their great
untidy wings beating in the air with a sound like gigantic
blacksmiths' bellows.

Although some 400 species of birds inhabit the African rain-
forest, their total population there is much less than that of the
savannas. Since there is little food for seed eaters, most feed on
insects and soft fruit and nectar, and the great majority are
small, for large species can only live on the ground or in the
canopy. The most remarkable among the latter is the palmnut
vulture which nests at heights of from 30 to 180 feet in the
Congo Forest. For seven weeks its single nestling is fed solely on
husks of palm seed, and then on palm fruit for a further four
weeks after it fledges. Yet it subsequently becomes a predator on
lizards and young monkeys, and also a carrion eater.

The birds themselves and their nestlings are preyed on by
snakes and monkeys, and seek to evade these predators in
various ingenious ways. The red-vented malimbe, one of the
weaver birds, for example, weaves strips of leaves into a spherical nest a few inches in diameter, but designs the entrance to
this in the form of a delicate pendent tube 4 inches wide and as

much as 2 feet long, which it fashions out of palm-fruit sheath-
ing. Presumably if a snake attempts to enter the nest, the tube
breaks off. By contrast, the male hornbill seals his mate into her
nesting-hole, 50 or 100 feet up a tree, with a mud plaster often
composed of termitary "concrete" softened with saliva, leaving
only a thin slit, too narrow for any predator to enter, through
which he can convey food to her; and some hornbills actually
molt and grow new feathers during a confinement that can extend to four months before they ultimately break out when the
young are ready to fledge. This confinement is, however, voluntary: for the female can break out if the male is killed and, in
some instances, invariably does so before the young fledge, leaving them to plaster up the nest-wall again.

Civet cats, golden cats and genets, being small with long bal-
ancing tails, are the predators in the canopy, while the stump-
tailed pottos and angwantibos—Africa's nearest relatives to the
unique lemurs of Madagascar—climb slowly and deliberately
through the treetops in search of insects, fruit and leaves, seldom letting go of a branch with more than one foot at a time,
and sleeping by day with hands and feet grasping the branch,
and forehead resting on it between the forelegs. If their forest is
destroyed, they die with it. Though no larger than tom-cats
they could be described as the sloths of Africa, for powerful
muscles in their forelimbs give their long opposable fingers and
toes a vice-like grip. So sluggish in their movements; lacking any
protective armor, though they exude a pungent secretion when
alarmed; and never voluntarily descending to the ground where
they are almost helpless, one wonders how they escape predators. However, the vertebrae on a potto's neck protrude through
the skin in a row of blunt spiny projections, concealed in the
woolly fur, and it is reputed, when attacked, to duck its head
between its forelegs, with the result that its assailant mouths a

row of spikes; or alternatively, to clasp its minute hands behind its bull-neck and jerk back the latter sharply. Though so small, it is amazingly strong, with a bull-dog grip in its very sharp canines. By contrast, the still smaller, nocturnally croaking galagos or bush-babies, with hind legs longer than front, can make standing jumps of 10 feet from branch to branch and leap 30 feet from tree to tree, while minute suction-pads on hands and feet assist them when they are clambering about the twigs.

The bush-baby is further equipped with a long claw on one finger for winkling out grubs from bark crevices. Perhaps, like the striped possum of the New Guinea and Queensland rain-forest, it locates the grub in the first place by drumming rapidly with slender, vibrating fingers along a rotten branch until it detects a gallery either by its hollow timbre or by the sound or vibrations made by a grub tunneling, and then prizes off the bark with its teeth. On the other hand the cat-sized aye-aye of Madagascan forests, the only other animal to have developed a long middle finger with a hook-like claw, was never observed by Jean Jacques Petter actually to extract a grub, although he watched them for hours working at minuscule larvae in the interior of the pits of terminolia fruits. Instead: "The fruit and the very hard pit were rapidly gnawed off at one end with the incisors, and the third digit was then thrust several times in rapid succession into the hole made in the almond and finally licked."

The tree hyrax, the only hoofed animal to have adapted itself to arboreal life, despite the fact that it has claws only on the inner toes of its hind-feet, also makes use of a suction device for climbing vertical trunks. This depends on flexor muscles which draw up the thickly padded, tuberculated soles of the hyrax's feet, thus creating a partial vacuum between these cups or disks and the trunk. The raucous howling of the male hyraxes from treetop to treetop is the most frequent night sound of the African jungle, always excepting the incessant rasping zither of the cicadas—produced by a flexible notched rib under the second wing—whose intolerable powerhouse hum or circular-saw screeching swells ear-splittingly and then diminishes with an unmusical but rhythmic cadence. The hyrax "serenade" is variously described as opening with a series of deep grunts or with a soft though piercing whistle repeated at regular intervals, but then the whistles gradually become shriller and shriller and more and more rapidly reiterated, until they almost merge into one; finally, just as the animal has worked itself up to its top note and most frenzied repetition, it ends abruptly with a shriek as if cut short with a knife.

The 4-foot-long tree pangolins are almost exclusively arboreal, descending to the ground only infrequently at night. Pangolins—those elongated armadillos—have been described as mammals disguised as saurians, for their bodies and very long tails are armored with horny, leaf-shaped, sharp-edged and overlapping scales inserted into the skin by one edge and erectable like a bird's feathers; only the face and narrow toothless muzzle, the ventral parts and the inner surface of the feet are unprotected. If a tree pangolin, hanging from a branch by the bare underside of its prehensile tail, is threatened by a predator, special muscles enable it to roll up swiftly into a ball, with head and legs covered by its tail. In this posture no predator can attack its vulnerable soft belly. So powerful are these muscles that a pangolin can hold its body at right-angles to a vertical trunk by the grip of its hind-feet and the pressure of its flattened tail. Its 6-foot-long relative, the giant pangolin or scaly ant-eater, whose recurved claws oblige it to progress on the ground in short shuffling hops on its in-turned knuckles, also has this ability to roll up protectively.

Tree pangolins clamber about the branches almost as ef-

Tree pangolin

ficiently as lizards in search of the ferocious small black tree ants and the spherical nests of termites, preferably those of young colonies. These they probably locate with their constantly exploring noses and quivering nostrils for, being nocturnal, their eyes are only pea-sized, though it is true that they also have acute hearing, rolling up instantly at the crushing of a dead leaf underfoot. Breaking open a nest with its immense hooked claws, the pangolin thrusts its long worm-like tongue deep into the galleries and withdraws it thickly coated with termites adhering to its sticky mucus, though why the soil and debris within the termitary does not also adhere to its tongue is inexplicable. Although the pangolins' geographical range may be determined by the presence or absence of termites—their northern limits, the Yangtze in south-east China, coincides with that of two species of termites—they also feed on ponerines and driver ants, from whose stings or bites they are protected by the copious secretions of mucus in their mouths, throats and stomachs, except when the latter are in their most belligerent nomadic phases, when even pangolins must retreat or coil up.

The rain-forest is an unsuitable habitat for large herds of grazing ungulates, because of the density of the trees and the almost total lack of grass. It is a sanctuary for browsers and fruit eaters in ones and twos and family groups such as pygmy antelopes with delicate hooves no larger than a man's fingernail, and small dik-diks and duikers, feeding silently and mainly at night on fallen fruits and the leaves and young shoots of selected shrubs. With rounded muzzle, short neck, backward-pointing horns and low forequarters, a duiker (the Africaans "diver") slips through the shrubbery with a minimum of effort, eluding the hunting leopard by agility rather than speed, twisting and turning as it weaves through the densest undergrowth, a barely detectable gray or brown form.

Deep in the dark and humid forest of the eastern Congo there is abundant forage for pairs or solitary okapi which, unlike the small red buffalo, forest hogs and elephants, do not inhabit the dense tangle of leafy jungle, but during the greater part of the day keep to well-drained ridges and higher ground near streams, where the trees are biggest and a dim religious light and dripping moisture prevail beneath the vast leafy canopy, and the cathedral-like silence is broken only by noisy-winged hornbills and the weird shouts of chimpanzees. Here the undergrowth is thin and scanty, and faint twisting trails score the forest floor. Along such trails the okapi browses on leaves and the young shoots of many kinds of shrubs and trees, exploiting its own special food niche through the medium of its long neck and 14-inch tongue (only 4 inches shorter than a giraffe's), which is prehensile, enabling it to grasp and pull down branches and strip them of their leaves and, incidentally, to flick flies from its withers and clean its enormous ears; a feature it shares with the bongo in a habitat where ears are more efficient than eyes. Its chocolate or purplish-red color, disrupted by stripes on its hindquarters, is an effective camouflage; and the naturalist Cuthbert Christy, who collected for museums for twenty-five years, mainly in the Congo's legendary Ituri Forest, describes how he twice encountered okapi at distances of less than 30 yards in dark forest, but could see only the white markings on their faces and legs, and did not recognize these as belonging to any animal until the okapi bolted.

The large 420-pound bongo's bright chestnut-red is also disrupted by mottled ears, a white chevron on the forehead, white cheek spots, a white crescent on the chest and, like the eland of the savanna, by ten or thirteen narrow transverse white stripes across back and sides. But, unlike the solitary okapi, the bongos associate in family groups of ten or a dozen or more

Okapi

members when lying up in the thickest fastnesses of the bamboo forest, though feeding solitarily on young bamboo shoots, lobelias, nettles and ripe fruit, tree roots, rooting wood fiber and the pungent bark of fallen trees. Despite their large size and their 3-foot-long, lyre-shaped horns they torpedo their way through the densest tangle, negotiating gaps beneath fallen trunks that appear too small even for a duiker's passage, and open up deep trails converging on streams. Although often living at considerable altitudes, they frequent especially those outlying strips of gallery forest that occur at varying levels in tropical Africa, either in low-lying areas bordering watercourses, swamp and grassland, or as montane belts between the high alpine moorlands and the savanna plateaus.

The inhabitants of the rain-forest assist in its regeneration. The pervasive odor of ripe and fermenting fruits attracts not only the antelopes, large and small, but rats, mice, squirrels, porcupines, hogs and elephants. Rats and squirrels carry away some of the fruits, and giant forest hogs and elephants swallow them whole and void the stones, while the herds of red river hogs or bush-pigs plough up large areas of scrub-jungle and secondary forest at night, especially while rooting for tubers and giant snails and among the tree roots in the soft earth banks of the innumerable small streams, whose clear shallow waters meander through the forest in intricate patterns. Seeds germinate quickly in the upturned soil.

Rich reddish-brown or vivid orange in color, with white ear-tassels, dorsal ridges of white and black hair, and short razor-sharp tusks capable of disemboweling a leopard, bush-pigs are the most spectacular of their kind. By contrast, the little-known giant forest hogs, which reach a length of 5 feet and weights of 280 or possibly 420 pounds, have hides of long, black erect bristles. These, being 6 or 7 inches long on the back of the head and forepart of the neck exaggerate the length and massiveness of the head, which is further distinguished by long up-curving tusks and huge warty grayish-white excrescences of thickened skin and gristle, resembling the fungal growth on trees, below their eyes. These excrescences, which must drastically diminish the hog's visual range, presumably have some masculine significance, for they are most exaggerated in the boar and may be absent in the immature sow. Despite their enormous snout-disks, more than 5 inches broad with huge, widely spaced nostrils, forest hogs are browsers, not rooters like other pigs, feeding mainly on tall grasses and leaves in swampier parts of the forest, and raiding native plantations on its outskirts. Although frequently in sounders of five or six, they are more often solitary or in pairs, and Fred Merfield, who hunted and collected for fifteen years in the remotest forests of the Cameroons, and was an observant naturalist, noted that when the sow is due to farrow she, like the bush-pig sow, heaps up a pile of leaves or matted vegetation and retreats beneath these, while the boar stands guard outside, attacking any man or beast that approaches.

The two largest mammals of the African rain-forest, the forest elephants and the forest buffalo or bush-cows, also tend to associate in groups rather than in herds. The latter are almost as wary and difficult to approach as okapi, bolting at great speed through or, like forest hogs, beneath the dense undergrowth, unhampered by their short horns that point nearly directly backwards. Both they and the elephants are smaller than their counterparts in the savannas, though the red bush-cows exhibit varying degrees of interbreeding with the gigantic black savanna buffalo whose calves, significantly, are brick-red. Pockets of the true forest elephant—though apparently no pygmy race, as was formerly believed—exist today in parts of Nigeria and Ghana and from the Congo to western Uganda. The majority probably differ in certain physical respects from the savanna or bush elephants, though it is impossible to find two authorities in total agreement on these distinctions; but, as a general rule, it can be stated that forest elephants average less than 8 feet at the shoulder, with the largest bulls not exceeding 9½ feet and 3 tons in weight: whereas bush elephants average more than 8 feet, with the largest bulls standing 11½ feet or exceptionally 13 feet and weighing 7 tons or more. The ears of true forest elephants are relatively small and rounded in comparison with the large triangular-shaped ears of the bush elephants; and some have a considerable growth of hair, in contrast to the very sparse hair of the bush elephants. But, like the buffalo, both interbreed where they co-exist, and probably do not constitute true subspecies. However, the *natural* habitat of all elephants is rain-forest and the dense gallery-forests, and it has been suggested that possibly a third of Africa's present population of about 300,000 elephants still inhabit the Congo, with the largest concentration in the heart of the rain-forest. There, they live in loose associations of families forming herds about 100 strong, whereas herds of bush elephants may be 500 or 1,000 strong, though when feed is scarce these break up into smaller groups that maintain contact by smell.

Rain-forest provides elephants with three essentials—an abundant supply of water, luxuriant vegetation, and shade. With their thick hides and greater or lesser degree of hair covering, both African and Asiatic elephants can tolerate extreme heat or extreme cold. The former indeed climb above the snow-line to an altitude of 15,000 feet on Mt. Kenya, possibly when in search of such special foods as the medicinal berries of the mu-kaita tree. But both are vulnerable to sunstroke, which has been known to cause paralysis of the trunk in Asiatic elephants, and the trained forestry elephants in the former Belgian Congo habitually covered their heads with grass, leaves and wet soil if they were not provided with hats. Under natural conditions elephants venture out of the forest only in the early morning, at dusk and during the night. In the heat of the day they rest in the shade, cooling themselves by flapping their colossal ears, which may be 6 feet long and 5 feet across; and any injury preventing this punkah movement of the ears, with their complex network of blood vessels, may seriously affect body-heat control.

An elephant requires from 30 to 50 gallons of water a day; and whether or not Africa was formerly much wetter than it is today, it was certainly much more widely and extensively forested, and elephants were to be found wherever there was, firstly, water and, secondly, forest. Some herds indeed became permanent inhabitants of swampy regions such as Lake Chad, adapting themselves to a true semi-aquatic existence, for elephants are excellent swimmers and the forest herds pass much of their time in deep water and even in fast-flowing rivers, regulating the depth at which they float by swallowing air or water. Young ones may even dive, though normally they lower themselves until only the top of the head and the eyes are above water, while the S-shaped trunk serves as a breathing tube. The total disappearance of elephants from Africa north of the Sahara, within the past 2,000 years, must be attributed to the loss of surface water and the destruction of the forests.

Rain-forest also provides elephants with a full range of essential foods including arboreal fruits, leaves, buds, twigs, branches, wood fibers and flowering vines, and roots and tubers, together with some monocotyledonous material such as the shoots, leaves and stems of bamboo, and finally salt-licks. If the latter are in swampy ground the elephant digs out the soil with his tusks and then stirs it up in the water and drinks the mixture; if the salt soil is dry, he "vacuums" up small quantities with his trunk and blows it into his mouth. Innumerable trails lead through the forest to salt-licks: "Pigs come both by night and day to excavate in them . . . and to wallow in the mudholes beneath them," wrote Christy. "Elephants will spend the whole night by them, making great grooves in the bank with their tusks. Buffalos leave the marks of their horns. During the daytime monkeys come in scores, getting right to the back of the holes, and scraping out pieces of the hard, light-coloured earth with their fingers and teeth. I have sometimes seen fifty or a hundred monkeys, chiefly Colobus, round the salt-licks."

In their natural habitat elephants are primarily browsers of arboreal plants and shrubs, though bundles of herbs and grasses are uprooted intact with a winding movement of the trunk and then leisurely knocked against a forefoot or the underside of the trunk to remove the soil, before being placed crosswise in the mouth and the juicy mid-portion bitten through: "Who cannot experience a sense of timeless peace watching a huge elephant, apparently meditative, gently slapping a delicate, flowering herbaceous plant . . . bruising it just sufficiently to elicit the sweetest scent and most delicious flavour?", writes Sylvia Sikes, educational missionary, zoology lecturer, elephant hunter and author of the most up-to-date monograph on the African elephant, to which I am indebted for much of this account. She describes how, when confronted by a large tree, perhaps 30 feet tall and 2 feet in diameter, bearing fruit or nuts, green leaves or palatable bark, an elephant first cleans up all the fallen fruit and then, having tested the bole with his trunk, puts his forehead against it and pushes. If the tree stands firm he may then coil his trunk round it and, bracing his tusks against it, shake vigorously, displacing some of the fruits. Alternatively, if he feels the tree yielding at his initial push, he may continue to pressure it, butting with head and pushing with foreleg alternately, until he actually uproots it or until the bole ultimately snaps. Trees with heavy crowns, like acacias, have surface roots, and Christy observed that "by simply pushing with his forehead and the protruded basal portion of the trunk, with occasional assistance from a forefoot, and getting the tree on the swing, an elephant is able to bring it down. Other trees, even deep-rooted ones forty feet high, he frequently fells in the same way, often exposing and severing some of the roots with his tusks."

An elephant will labor in this way for hours in order to obtain some favorite fruit. Individual berries and buds are plucked with the tip of the trunk, and branches are pulled off and broken into small pieces with the trunk, but never, curiously enough, by a combination of trunk and forefoot in the manner of an Asiatic elephant, though ripe coconuts are opened by gentle pressure with a forefoot, which fractures husk and shell without crushing the meat. The elephant's diminutive relative, the tree hyrax, is reputed, incidentally, to be the only other animal capable of cracking the raphia palm nut with its very strong jaws. To procure the sweet, though tannin-astringent bark of an acacia thorn, an elephant gashes the bole with a tusk, or splits it by pressure from his forehead, prises up the bark, and tears it off in long strips with his trunk—an operation that leaves the favorite ironwood tree vulnerable to fire.

An African bull elephant consumes about 5 per cent of its weight in vegetation daily, and to obtain this massive quantity of fodder must spend 16 or 20 hours out of the 24 in browsing. Thus, during the growing and fruiting seasons the original herds were continually on the move to fresh feeding grounds, traveling out of the forest on to the then well-wooded though more open savannas; or to swampy areas which offered the additional attraction of refuge from the heat of the sun; and also undertaking long migrations, involving considerable changes in altitude, to localities containing such favorite foods as the plum-like fruit of the merula. Indeed, according to Ivan Sanderson, a herd might pass ten years on a continuous migration on a more or less oblong circuit before returning to its original starting place. Tropical Africa is a network of pathways and trails, but not all of them are man-made, and Christy observed that:

> In an elephant country one frequently has occasion to marvel at the ramifications of the elaborate system of roads and pathways made and kept up by the elephant community. Main highways from two to three feet wide run for scores of miles across the country through forest and bush. These elephant roads are rammed too hard by countless feet for anything to grow upon them. In the dry season for many miles at a

stretch they are smooth enough for a bicycle track. . . . Only in the forest are they poached up so as to make travelling along them difficult. Some are probably hundreds of years old, to judge by the way rocky banks of rivers . . . are worn down and deeply indented by them. Lesser ways, branch tracks and short cuts lead off, not simply here, there and anywhere, but converging upon river crossings or outlying blocks of forest, or continuing as highways direct to other parts of the country.

Sylvia Sikes has described how:

Mating, calving and the early rearing of the young normally took place in the vicinity of abundant supplies of surface water and of cool shady groves, thickets, in deep jungle, gallery forests and swamp forests. This period usually coincided with the prevailing dry season or seasons. As the dry season ended, the clouds began to gather and the first storms to break, the elephants became restive and started to move in their family units and clans towards the neighbouring, more open, savanna woodland. In all parts of Africa, just before the rainy season begins, deciduous trees lose their leaves—but, within a couple of weeks, and before the onset of the first storms, new buds burst forth and the dry ground springs into life with innumerable flowering herbs and fresh green grass and foliage. This was the season when the . . . elephants moved out into more open country. As the first storms broke and the dry pools and gulleys filled with rushing, muddy torrents, there was adequate water for drinking and wallowing. The clouds billowed across the sky, hiding the glaring sun for several hours daily, the humidity and air temperature were high and the vegetation tasty and palatable.

But with the widespread destruction of their forest environment, large numbers of African elephants were forced to become semi-permanent or even permanent inhabitants of the savannas. Today, with the ever-increasing despoliation of natural

Africa, thousands of elephants are not only obliged to feed mainly on grass, but are almost totally exposed without shade to the tropical sun for all of every day throughout the year. Sylvia Sikes suggests that this exposure may, ironically, prove to be a limiting factor to the size of the herds in the over-exploited national parks, since its effects will be greatest on the younger and weaker elephants, forced out by the older and stronger beasts to the perimeter of what patches of shade are available. Within the restricted boundaries of the parks the elephants may be literally eating themselves out of house and home and laying waste what must eventually be their last refuge. Even under natural conditions elephants are wasteful feeders with inefficient digestive systems, destroying more than they eat; but although a locality in which a herd has been feeding for several weeks has been likened to a battlefield, with only the tough tamarind trees undamaged, there is normally little trampling done or uprooting of trees not directly connected with feeding. In the bountiful and luxuriant rain-forest the temporary destruction of a block here and another there in the endless mass of trees was of no account ecologically. On the contrary, the elephants' wastage enriched the forest soil, provided fruits and insects for monkeys and birds attracted by the upheaval among the trees and shrubbery, and assisted in controlling the extravagant burgeoning of the tropical forest. But when, as in Uganda, the elephants' share of an entire country is reduced by encroaching cultivation and livestock from 70 per cent to 17 per cent in thirty years—during which period a herd is potentially capable of doubling its numbers—and that share is composed mainly of forest reserves, national parks and sleeping-sickness zones, then, as W. J. Eggeling has pointed out, the protective screen of bush around the remaining forests is so battered and broken by hungry elephants that dry-season fires on the savannas sweep right up to the edge of the

forest, destroying young trees colonizing the screen and scorch-
ing the bases of the mature trees. In the vicinity of much
frequented water-holes, isolated forests steadily decrease in size,
and elephants, not fire, become the controlling factor in the life
of a forest.

11: The Noisy World of Chimpanzees

There are some thirty species of monkeys in the African rain-forest—silver monkeys with black faces framed by a white band of hair; fruit-eaters, such as the vervet monkeys and the small red-tail monkeys; and leaf-eaters, such as the colubuses, with complex stomachs enabling them to extract the maximum nourishment from their limited diet. The large red colobuses, with long, heavy hanging tails and coal-black and rich chestnut-red fur that gleams in the morning sun as if burnished, range widely through the upper canopy in troops of sixty or more. The black-and-white colobuses, with black faces framed by white fur, fleecy white mantles around their shoulders and over their backs, and long black tails with white tassels, are even more agile than the red colobuses, leaping 30 feet from tree to tree, running down trunks headfirst, or hurling themselves from the tops of 150-foot trees, to crash into the branches below. Their prolonged and reverberating hollow croakings, repeated as many as fifty times, are one of the first sounds to be heard from the awakening forest just before dawn, if no chimpanzees are present. On the forest floor, though sleeping in the trees, are immense troops of olive baboons digging up roots and chewing the pithy stems of shrubs, or smaller troops of the omnivorous drills and mandrills, which supplement their plant and root food with insects, worms, snails, frogs, lizards, snakes and small mammals. Whether or not the notoriously lurid coloring of the mandrills' bare facial skin and buttocks serves as a visual aid to contact in the forest twilight, as has been suggested, it certainly plays a role in threat display between males, when their chests also turn blue, and red spots appear on their wrists and ankles, while the colorful buttocks are presented in submissive gestures to dominant males.

Monkeys and baboons, blue duiker browsing near the ground on the lowest vegetational level of young leaves, red duiker browsing taller shrubs, and bushbuck at a still higher level, the forest buffalo and elephants, leopards—these are some of the associates of the chimpanzees, whose world range extends over several hundred thousand square miles of rain-forest on either side of the equator from Upper Guinea and the Congo to the East African lakes, though they actually inhabit perhaps only one-quarter or one-fifth of this vast area and are divided into two races. A so-called pygmy race, rather smaller on average and including many individuals distinguished by the presence of a membrane partially linking their second and third toes, is isolated in a region of remote forests between the Congo and Kasia rivers. The latter form an impassable barrier, because chimpanzees, like all apes and most monkeys, though the West African debrazza monkey is a voluntary and excellent swimmer, dislike water. Though capable, even when carrying young on their backs, of leaping over 6-foot-wide streams from a bipedal standing start on soft ground, chimps usually cross streams only where natural bridges are available, and even make use of fallen trunks to detour round shallow pools.

Since apparently nothing is known about the habits of the

pygmy race this chapter will be solely concerned with the common chimpanzees, whose habitat probably extends upwards to the tree-limit at 10,000 or 11,000 feet on such mountains as Ruwenzori, though a minority have left the rain-forest and colonized the more open deciduous woodlands on the eastern slopes of Lake Tanganyika, where they experience rather different climatic conditions that include a dry season from June to September, and a wet season with heavy rain on most days from October to May.

It is only within the past fifteen years that any intensive field study of chimpanzees has been undertaken, primarily by Jane Goodall (now Jane van Lawick-Goodall), who began watching them in 1960 in what is today the Gombe Stream Reserve east of Lake Tanganyika, and whose initial account of her experiences alone in the forest is described in an entrancing book, *In the Shadow of Man;* and also by Vernon Reynolds and his wife, who lived for eight months in 1964 in the Budongo Forest in Uganda, and whose book *Budongo* is hardly less enthralling. Jane Goodall, however, established an unique relationship with numbers of individual chimps by patiently winning their complete confidence and daily friendship, which culminated in adult males allowing her to groom them, as if she were another member of the group; though this extraordinary status was only achieved after months of fear and retreat on their part, followed by a bolder period of aggression and hostility when the males shook branches at her and attempted to frighten her away by charging. The American, Adriaan Kortlandt has also made a number of expeditions since 1960 to the Belgian Congo to study chimpanzees; and a comparison of these various accounts of the same species of animal in three different environments has sometimes suggested three different kinds of animals.

The Budongo Forest's 135 square miles of almost continuous

canopy, south of the Murchison National Park and on the escarpment above Lake Albert, is typical chimpanzee country. For 250 miles to the south of it isolated stands of forest, separated by as much as 15 miles of cultivated land and barren hills, are also inhabited by chimps. The most southerly of these, lying just within the territories of Congo and Rwanda, is Impenetrable Forest (Kayonza), the only known forest in which chimps and gorillas inhabit the same ridge. Reynolds estimated that the chimpanzee population of Budongo, together with the 35 square miles of swampy region known as Siba, was probably between 1,000 and 2,000: whereas between 100 and 150 occupied the 22½ square miles that were habitable for them in the Gombe Stream Reserve.

Under normal conditions small groups of chimps scatter over 6 or 8 square miles of jungle during their incessant search for food, joining forces casually from time to time without hostility in large groups of 40 or 50 or as many as 75 when quantities of fruit are ripening in one particular locality. The composition of a group may change almost daily, as individuals wander away on their own in search of fruiting trees, and groups may interchange adult males and, less often, adult females. A group may indeed be composed solely of adult males for a period of two weeks. But groups do tend towards too differing social structures, with one consisting mainly of adult males and barren females, and the other of mothers and juveniles accompanied by one or two adult males. Juveniles remain with their mothers until four or five years old, and may even be suckled by them at that age and jump on their backs when danger threatens. Although a male chimp is fully mature when seven or eight he weighs only 40 pounds at that age, and not until he is thirteen or fifteen years old will he be accepted as a member of the adult hierarchy of males weighing 100 or 110 pounds. Nevertheless,

Jane Goodall's long and close association with the Gombe Stream chimps enabled her to establish the fact that every group has its dominant male, though for the most part he remains on friendly terms with the other males in the group, and does not even object to them mating with his favorite female; nor does he persecute any aged male too feeble to climb trees or to take part in the group's frequent individual or communal intimidation displays. So too, a group of sub-adult males may display a touching affection for a decrepit female and center their activities round her.

The search for food controls almost every aspect of the chimpanzees' daily and seasonal lives. The Budongo chimps forage and feed for six to eight hours of every twelve hours of the equatorial day and, like monkeys, sleep for the remaining twelve hours. They are equally at home on the ground or in the trees, but in both the Budongo Forest and the Gombe Stream Reserve between half and three-quarters of the hours of daylight are spent in the trees, where 90 per cent of their food is obtained. In the Belgian Congo, however, where Kortlandt's group procured much of their food from a plantation of paw-paws and bananas at the edge of the forest, he observed that they avoided all unnecessary climbing, walking from tree to tree and maintaining an elaborate road system in the forest bordering the plantation; and he adds that chimps living in sparsely wooded savannas in uninhabited regions often walk long distances from one grove of trees to the next. On the ground, and also on broad branches, chimps usually move about in a quadrupedal manner on the knuckles of their clenched hands and hind-feet flat on the ground; but in the open paw-paw plantation they frequently walked or ran bipedally for up to nine paces, without apparently experiencing any difficulty in retaining their balance before dropping on to all-fours again, thereby leaving their hands free

Chimpanzee

to carry the melon-sized paw-paws, and also extending their field of view in this potentially dangerous inhabited area.

In the trees chimps are agile and confident climbers, despite their lack of tails, swarming up smooth branchless trunks by clasping as far round as they can with their long arms and moving each hand up alternately while thrusting upwards with their legs; working out along slender branches, to hang by one hand over a 150-foot drop while plucking a fruit with the other hand; "brachiating" like gibbons and spider monkeys with hands clinging to a branch above their heads, feet dangling, and body swinging forwards, backwards, and to each side in turn, as arms move alternately; or swinging 10 or 20 feet through the air from tree to tree in gallery-forest, in which the interwoven canopy is not, as in the true rain-forest, disrupted by the emergent crowns of giant trees. Nevertheless, fractured bones are a common condition among chimpanzees, as they are among gorillas and gibbons, though not perhaps orangutans; but, unlike the other apes, chimps do not suffer from arthritis.

Chimps also sleep high up in the trees, constructing new "nests" every night, usually at a height of 30 or 40 feet where the branches are most pliable, though some nests are as low as 10 feet or as high as 150 feet. Whether or not such a large animal as a chimp could keep its balance in the crotch of a tree while sleeping, a crude nest-platform is obviously more comfortable than the soggy ground of the rain-forest. In the dry season those in the Gombe Reserve usually rested on the ground at midday, but when this was sodden in the wet season some constructed quite elaborate ground nests on which to sit hunched up with arms round knees and heads bowed until the rain stopped. Monkeys, being provided, like a small minority of chimpanzees and gorillas, with "sitting pads" in the form of bony growths on their buttocks, do not make sleeping nests, but all the apes, except the monkey-like gibbons, do; and this is also the habit of the sun bears of Malaya, Sumatra and Borneo.

During the last hour of daylight the chimpanzees feed industriously, but when the temperature drops sharply as the sun

sets, and cicadas begin chirping and hornbills wing their rasping
way to their roosting trees outside the forest, they move off in
threes and fours in search of suitable nesting-trees, though each
party keeps within sight of the others and infants sleep with
their mothers. A firm foundation, such as an upright fork or
crotch or two horizontal branches, is essential; and Reynolds
watched one chimp's nest-building technique, after it had
climbed a sapling but, finding it unsuitable, had climbed down
again and selected a larger tree:

> Sitting on the main branch, he pulled in surrounding leafy
> branches, working his way round in a circle and intertwining
> the branches, holding them in place beneath his feet. He did
> not break them off completely but just snapped them half
> through so that their resilience was gone but they were still
> firmly attached to the tree. After he had used every available
> branch at the site, his nest was still patchy, so he collected
> more branches from nearby, breaking them off this time, and
> laid them on top, or wove them in a little, finally adding leafy
> twiglets to complete the big, firm structure. . . . He did all
> this in three or four minutes. Now followed a settling down
> period of from five to ten minutes during which he made final
> adjustments. Once he called out and was answered by a brief
> chorus of goodnight hoots . . . then it was pitch dark and all
> was still.

Since 90 per cent of the Budongo chimpanzees' food consists
of fruit—none of which are larger than apples, and the majority
much smaller—they probably rarely need to drink. Reynolds
indeed witnessed only one instance, when a chimp dipped its
hand into a tree bowl 100 feet above the ground and then, holding it above its head, allowed the water to drip into its protruded lips. Jane Goodall, however, watched one drinking from
a stream with its lips, while another fashioned a kind of cup out
of leaves, and others crushed leaves into "sponges," after first

chewing and crumpling these to render them more absorbent. Such sponges might also be employed to clean out the last smear of blood from the skull of a baboon they had killed, while handfuls of leaves were used to dab at wounds or to wipe dirt from their bodies, or as absorbents in cases of diarrhea.

The chimps' daily and seasonal routine, and also their social grouping, is governed by the fruiting cycles of various kinds of trees, and to a lesser degree by the incidence of dry and wet seasons. Whenever Reynolds succeeded in locating a party of chimps in the early days of his study, he found them eating the juicy yellow fruits of a species of fig tree known as *mukunyu*. This very large tree, whose exceptionally smooth, sandy-brown bark contrasts with its bright-green leaves and yellow fruits, usually grows in sunny locations and often on valley slopes. Reynolds describes how day after day they found large groups of fifteen or more chimps gathered on these trees: "Hooting and shouting loud and long as they stuffed great quantities of the figs into their mouths, chewed them up, two or three at a time, and swallowed them down into stomachs which already looked full to bursting, looking around the while for another nice little cluster with the pink blush of ripeness on the orange skins."

Fig trees also grow all along the lower reaches of the stream in the Gombe Reserve, and one year, when an abundant crop lasted for eight weeks, the chimps fed on figs every day, visiting the trees in big or small groups, singly or in pairs; and Jane Goodall observed that, before or after gorging on the figs, they consumed large quantities of small purple fruits which, like so many of the items in their diet, were as bitter and astringent as sloes or crab-apples. Figs contain many tiny but indigestible seeds in their soft edible pulp, and after a few hours of feasting the chimps' faeces consist of almost pure wads of these seeds. Thus, in their daily commutings through the forest, the chimps and other fig-eaters must play a major role in the distribution of fig trees; but although the latter probably contribute considerably to soil fertility, foresters throughout West Africa are attempting to kill off systematically all fig trees by a massive poisoning program because they do not make good timber and in order to improve the growth of mahoganies. Since the chimpanzees' staple food at one season of the year is figs, this program could seriously disrupt their seasonal routine.

In Budongo the fig crop is exhausted late in April, and there is no more jubilant hooting and shouting, for with no large fruiting trees to act as a focal point of attraction, the chimps must now split up into small groups, perhaps including no more than from two to six members, and disperse in search of food. Vocalizing is now restricted to contact calls from individuals plucking young leaves from the branch tips of saplings 10 or 12 feet high. They also separate into small units when, during exceptionally prolonged rains, they wander through the forest feeding on the "custard apples" of the mbula trees. In contrast to the rather small, permanently compact groups of gorillas, who can obtain food at ground-level almost anywhere in their habitat, or the large permanent groups of baboons, the flexible nature of the chimpanzees' social organization enables small groups and individuals to locate widely separated sources of food. But late in May the communal hooting begins again, when sizable groups of chimps gather to the year's second fruit feast—that of the, again, bitter and astringent yellow-orange fruits of the small gnarled ngrube trees, which are scattered through the forest. The third fruiting cycle occurs in swampy areas such as Siba, and is provided by the igeria tree, whose masses of fruit resemble small green plums, which turn reddish and finally deep purple as they ripen, and smell like turpentine. These the chimps collect indiscriminately, cramming both ripe and unripe into their mouths. The ripe are digested, the green ones voided whole, since chimps eat greedily and are not particular as to whether or not they spit out the ¾-inch stones. The fourth cycle, lasting from the end of July until the middle of September, is that of the musisi, whose branches are festooned with thousands of small green, yellow or black fruits, depending upon their state of ripeness. This is one of the chief colonizing trees of the rain-forest, for its stones are excreted not only by chimps, but by blue and red-tail monkeys, civet cats, duikers and hornbills. Finally, in October the cycle begins all over again with fresh fruit on the fig trees.

During the musisi fruiting cycle in the Budongo Forest as many as sixty or eighty chimpanzees might be concentrated in an acre or two of these trees, though they frequently split up after their morning feast—their most active feeding period immediately after leaving their sleeping nests—but returned in the evening for another feast. At the end of his eight months' study Reynolds concluded that:

> While each region of six to eight square miles contained sixty to eighty chimpanzees which lived in that region and were able to find within that region a year-round food supply, nevertheless some of these individuals, mainly the adult males and females, did move freely from one region to another. . . . As the year had gone by and different species of trees had fruited, different parts of each region had been the focus of the chimpanzee attention, but we knew each region to contain a sufficiency of every fruit tree utilised by the chimpanzees, and so we had no reason to suppose that the *bulk* of the population of one region would ever leave it and go to another.

In the Gombe Stream Reserve more than ninety species of trees and plants have been identified as chimpanzee food sources, and these include more than fifty kinds of fruits and more than thirty kinds of leaves and leaf-buds. But these by no means exhaust the chimps' food reserves. When fruit is scarce they lick the resin from tree trunks and chew dead wood-fiber and also bark and pith, spitting out round wads of these after a few minutes' mastication; they eat the leaves and the plum-sized red fruits of the juicy green aframomum shrub, and peel and chew the stems of another juicy shrub, the marantochloa; and, avoiding the swamp-growing rattan's needle-sharp spines, break off smooth lengths that can be peeled, and chew these, as if sticks of sugar-cane, while on the move through the trees. Birds' eggs and nestlings, termites and ants in large numbers, caterpillars, the grubs of bees, wasps and gall-flies, and honeycomb are also eaten, and obtained with some ingenuity. On one occasion Fred Merfield came upon six chimpanzees at the edge of a small clearing, sitting in a circle around a nest of small black bees, engaged in poking long twigs down the entrance hole and withdrawing them coated with honey: either taking turns to do so or seizing twigs from one another. A similar technique is employed for catching termites during the Gombe Reserve season of short rains from October to January, when the princes and princesses are swarming out of the termitaries for their nuptial flights. After first scratching open one of a termitary's sealed exits with thumb or forefinger, a chimp carefully pokes along grass or vine stem or twig stripped of its leaves down the hole; the termites cling to the stem as it is withdrawn, and the chimp dislodges them by pulling the stem through his lips. Adult chimps possess the patience to "fish" for termites for two or three hours at a time, biting off the ends of their tools when they become blunted or reversing them or discarding them in favor of fresh ones from the three or four spares they have previously placed beside them. Tools are also employed to capture ants, including the tree-nesting *Oecophylla* and the driver ants. In dealing with the latter, a chimp uses a stick, both to stir up the underground nest and also in an attempt to prevent the soldiers from crawling over him. Sticks are also used to procure ants from those hard football-sized nests that are constructed around branches; to enlarge entrances to underground bees' nests, enabling the chimp to insert his hand and pull out a section of honeycomb, apparently indifferent to the bees' activities; to detect grubs in dead wood by probing holes and then sniffing at the end of the stick; and to investigate any unusual object such as a dead python; while in West Africa chimps have been reported using rocks to break open palm-nut kernels.

In the Gombe Stream Reserve, and perhaps in other similar habitats, chimpanzees exhibit carnivorous tendencies. Although Jane Goodall's study group of as many as fifty-eight chimps sometimes wandered away from the Reserve there was never any apparent seasonal food scarcity and, as we have seen, at least ninety different kinds of fruits and plants were available to them. It is therefore difficult to accept the hypothesis that "savanna" chimps are carnivorous because vegetable food is less abundant than in the rain-forest. All one can say is that Jane Goodall noted that this craving for animal flesh appeared to occur in cycles which lasted for a month or two, that leaves were chewed after each bite of meat, and that most actual killings were the work of adolescent males, though other males in the group would position themselves, usually unsuccessfully, to cut off a potential victim's escape. She estimated that a group of forty chimps might kill more than twenty animals in the course of a year, including small antelope, young bushbuck and bush-pigs, red-tail and blue monkeys, young baboons and young and small adult red colobuses, though a large colobus is capable, when enraged, of putting a chimpanzee to flight. There were also two instances of native babies being killed near the Reserve.

Although chimpanzees are immensely strong it is inexplicable that such normally aggressive and domineering animals as baboons should make no attempt to attack a chimp holding a screaming infant baboon, particularly since groups of baboons sometimes attack groups of chimpanzees, though without serious injuries being inflicted by either side. The fact that Jane Goodall established a banana feeding place for her group of chimps, of which the baboons also took advantage, probably accounts for the unnaturally close contact between the two species in the Gombe Reserve; for while they might quarrel over the bananas—with the chimps leaping up and down and waving their arms and barking, and also throwing rocks and branches, usually inaccurately, at the baboons, before eventually retreating—curious friendships were formed, more especially between young animals. One between two young females lasted for about a year, while an old male baboon persistently and successfully importuned young chimps to groom him. In the Budongo Forest, however, although blue and red-tail monkeys often fed within a few feet of chimps in the same fruit-trees, with a large male blue sometimes forming a semi-permanent association with them, and although individual baboons were allowed to approach to within 5 yards, the chimps would move away when a screeching troop of baboons arrived.

Chimpanzees, in marked contrast to gorillas, are noisy animals. One obvious reason for this dissimilarity is to be found in their different feeding techniques. By calling frequently, the chimps maintain contact when dispersed widely in search of food over large tracts of forest in which they cannot see one another, with the hooting and shouting of bands of adult males attracting the less exploratory females and young to good feeding areas; but they are also particularly noisy when large groups are concentrated in groves of heavily laden fruit-trees. Jane

Goodall has described the arrival of a party of chimps at a single isolated msulula tree, whose crop of small orange and red fruits provided them with food for ten days. First, one chimp pouted its lips and uttered a series of low, resonant "pant-hoots," as she terms their loud hooting calls linked by noisy intakes of breath. The hoots became louder and louder, rising almost to a scream, and were taken up by one chimp after another; but once they had begun feeding, they did so in silence. The discovery of trees bearing fruit creates tremendous excitement, as the following passage from her *In the Shadow of Man* illustrates:

> Often, as one group crossed the grassy ridge separating the Kasakela Valley from the fig trees in the home valley, the male chimpanzees . . . would break into a run . . . sometimes dragging a fallen branch, sometimes stamping or slapping on the hard earth. These charging displays were almost always accompanied by loud pant-hoots. . . . If there were chimps feeding in the fig trees they nearly always hooted back. . . . Then the new arrivals hurried down the steep slope and . . . the two groups met up in the fig trees. . . . I saw one female, newly arrived in a group, hurry up to a big male and hold her hand towards him . . . he reached out, clasped her hand in his, drew it towards him and kissed it with his lips. I saw two adult males embrace each other in greeting.

Kortlandt's chimps, whose group had a maximum strength of forty-eight, were more inhibited in their plantation environment. The males were always the first to approach their favorite patch of bananas and paw-paws, heralding their arrival with cries which grew in intensity as they got nearer. But when close to the clearing they would fall silent, and a broad black face would peep cautiously through the leaves. Then, after an interval, they would step out one by one from behind the bushes and trees, with at least one walking upright in order to obtain a better view over the open ground. But when they were satisfied that the plantation was deserted—though they appeared to be aware of Kortlandt's observation hides, some of which were placed at a height of 80 feet, if not of his actual presence—they broke out into a deafening display, shrieking and screaming, stamping on the ground with hands and feet or smacking tree trunks with one open hand, even pulling down half-grown paw-paw trees; and occasionally one would grab a branch and brandish it or hurl it while charging through the group. However, this was almost the only time that these particular chimps were noisy. Once they had begun feeding they communicated by gestures or by changes in facial expression or posture, while females with young ones were normally silent, wary and shy.

Natural phenomena also excite the chimps. Although individual males often react to the onset of heavy rain, Jane Goodall witnessed a mass group reaction on only three occasions over a period of ten years. One such display took place after she had been watching a group feeding in a great fig tree for a couple of hours. It had been gray and overcast during the morning, and at midday, when the first heavy drops of rain began to fall, the chimps climbed down from their tree and plodded up a steep grassy slope to an open ridge at the top of it. The storm broke just as they reached the ridge, with torrential rain and a sudden clap of thunder right overhead:

As if there was a signal, one of the big males stood upright and, as he swayed rhythmically from foot to foot, I could just hear the rising crescendo of his pant-hoots above the beating of the rain. Then he charged off, flat-out down the slope . . . some thirty yards and then swinging round the trunk of a small tree . . . leapt into the low branches and sat motionless.

Almost at once two other males charged after him. One of them broke off a branch from a tree as he ran and brandished it in the air before hurling it ahead of him. The other, as he reached the end of his run, stood upright and rhythmically swayed the branches of a tree back and forth, before seizing a huge bough. . . . A fourth male, as he too charged, leapt into a tree and, almost without breaking his speed, tore off a huge branch, leapt with it to the ground and continued down the slope. . . . As the males charged down and plodded back up, so the rain fell harder and harder, jagged forks or brilliant flares of lightning lit the leaden sky and the crashing of the thunder seemed to shake the very mountain.

Charging and intimidation displays, with hair bristling, are also activated by the discovery of a rich fruit tree, by a meeting with another group, or by frustration of some other emotional excitement associated with the presence of potential predators or undesirable intruders such as baboons or man, and also when a male challenges for the number one position in his group's masculine hierarchy. Sticks are, as already mentioned, habitually employed by chimps as tools, and their use in "rain-dances" or in intimidation display comes naturally to them. One male in the Gombe Stream group, referred to as Mike, achieved the number one position by persistently charging at the dominant male, Goliath, while dragging two or even three paraffin cans. These created such a terrifying din that Goliath was scared into actually leaving the Reserve for a couple of weeks. However, the leadership is not relinquished tamely, and Jane Goodall recounts how "One day . . . a series of distinctive rather melodious pant-hoots, with characteristic quavers at the close, announced the return of Goliath. . . . Mike responded immediately, hooting himself and charging across the clearing. Then he climbed a tree and sat staring over the valley every hair on end."

A few minutes later Goliath appeared and commenced one of his spectacular displays:

He must have seen Mike for he headed straight for him, dragging a huge branch. Then he leapt up into a tree near that of Mike and was still. For a moment Mike stared towards him and then he too began to display, swaying the branches of his tree, swinging to the ground, hurling a few rocks and, finally, climbing up into Goliath's tree and swaying the branches there. When he stopped Goliath immediately reciprocated . . . and for a few . . . moments both . . . were swaying branches within a few feet of each other. . . . But an instant later both . . . were on the ground, displaying. . . . Finally they stopped and sat, staring at each other. It was Goliath who moved next, standing upright as he rocked a sapling; when he paused, Mike charged past him, hurling a rock and drumming, with his feet, on the trunk of a tree.

This went on for nearly half an hour. . . . Yet . . . apart from occasionally hitting one another with the ends of the branches they swayed, neither . . . actually attacked the other. Suddenly, after an extra long pause . . . Goliath . . . rushed up to Mike . . . and began to groom him with feverish intensity [in submission]. For a few seconds Mike ignored Goliath . . . then he . . . with a vigour almost matching that of Goliath, began to groom his vanquished rival. And there they sat, grooming each other without a pause, for over an hour.

If any carnivore preys upon chimpanzees it can only be the large forest leopards; but, as Reynolds has suggested, the howling of a mob of chimps, whatever function it may have in the organization of their society, must be extremely intimidating even to a leopard. Their communal din can be heard at a distance of 2 miles, and is answered in kind by other chimps in the neighborhood with some of their more than twenty different vocalizations, including the dominant loud whoops which, as they grow more and more excited, rise to a shriek and culminate in a burst of drumming. Their howling is indeed a terrifying sound, described by Gerald Durrell in the dense forest of the Cameroons as a succession of blood-curdling screams followed by bursts of maniacal laughter that die away to a dreadful whimpering. A chimpanzee's blackness and appearance might also deter a leopard from attacking. Reynolds has described the scene at one of his earliest encounters with a group of chimps:

> A big black hairy arm . . . plucking fruits and stuffing them into a broad pink mouth. Farther back were others. . . . we could hear them snapping branches. From time to time they called and the din was terrific. . . . One saw us and suddenly the whole area was filled with a different cry, harsher and shriller; there were chimpanzees everywhere, swinging about in the tree-tops, crashing from branch to branch, diving down into the undergrowth and rushing off. As we talked, a fine rain seemed to be falling on us. We looked up and there . . . was a big adult male, with a balding head and grey rump, placidly peeing on us and looking down.

On a later encounter:

> A huge volley of hoots and hollers and howls and barks shattered the silence . . . and the ground shook with the noise of a deep base drum . . . close ahead in a sapling not ten yards away . . . was a young adult . . . staring at us fixedly. . . . At first he chewed leaves and then looked down at us, chewed some more and looked again. Then suddenly, he let out a harsh, shrill bark. He began to swing the sapling from side to side . . . then he leapt off it to the ground and immediately clambered up another even closer to us. And now the most amazing sight . . . appeared before us. . . . Chimp after chimp after chimp climbed up the saplings all round us, and up in the trees above our heads more and more of them appeared. They barked and shrieked with harsh cries. They shook branches. They leap about. . . . The chorus grew louder and louder. . . . Drumming boomed close beside us. . . . The shouting swelled again and I timed a chorus, which

went on for six minutes continuously, lulled for ten seconds, then swelled again.

Old hunters in the rain-forest alluded to chimpanzee "carnivals," which the native inhabitants referred to as *ngoma*, a term for dancing and drumming; and on one occasion when Reynolds was watching a group of a dozen chimpanzees in some igeria trees on the fringe of a swampy river in the Siba, he noticed that another group of similar strength was approaching, calling and drumming as it came. The latter suddenly climbed up into the first group's trees, whereupon *all* began the wildest screaming and hooting, while swinging about the trees, running along branches at top speed and leaping down branch by branch to the ground; only to climb up again and shake the branches wildly, stamping and slapping them, while occasionally closing up to each other briefly and parting again. And behind all this confusion a steady undercurrent of drumming reverberated in great rolls through the trees, fantastically loud, lunatic, frenzied. "For a minute or two this phenomenon, like a cyclone or passing express train, swept past us and then was gone."

These drumming and hooting carnivals can however continue for the whole of an afternoon, if not longer; and an adult male chimp in the act of drumming beats rhythmically with hands or feet on the flanking buttresses of various kinds of trees, though especially on those of the tall and slender ironwood trees which grow on the virgin soil in the deepest interiors of centuries-old rain-forest. Although the tropical forest floor may lie 60 or 70 feet above the underlying rock, most of the tree roots spread widely through the upper 18 inches only of fertile topsoil; and tap-roots, characteristic of temperate forests trees, are the exception. It is therefore reasonable to assume that buttress roots, in the form of numbers of broad-based fluted extensions from the lower part of the bole, serve to anchor the giant trees; though various arguments have been advanced against this assumption. The significant point is that these buttresses, which may extend for 27 feet up the trunk of a large tree and project outwards for almost as great a distance, are often harder than the trunk and, when struck with an axe, produce a peculiar hollow ringing sound.

According to Reynolds, the most efficient drum is provided by a buttress consisting of two planks parallel to each other and 6 or 9 inches apart. These form a kind of open box, the surface of which resounds with a crisp vibrating note when struck; and it is the latter, not the mechanical whack of the chimp's hand, that carries great distances through the forest. Drumming, like display, is often triggered off by emotional frustration and relieves tension, though no doubt, like hooting, it also serves to maintain contact between widely scattered groups and individuals. However, carnivals probably only occur when groups from two different localities meet and join forces at a common feeding ground for a few days before splitting up once more, having perhaps exchanged a few of their members.

12: The Home of the Mountain Gorillas

The African rain-forest is also the home of the world's only two races of the magnificent gorillas, whose respective habitats are separated by 650 miles of Congo forest. Possibly 50,000 gorillas of the western race—about which, like the pygmy chimpanzees, we know almost nothing—are scattered over an immense area of forested lowlands and hills lying mainly between the Congo and Niger rivers, and extending inland for some 500 miles to the vicinity of the Ubangi River, where Merfield found them very numerous forty or fifty years ago.

The eastern race, numbering between 5,000 and 15,000, is contained in an area of some 35,000 square miles of central Africa's remnants of less luxuriant rain-forest, though they actually occupy only about a quarter of this area, since their groups are concentrated in some sixty more or less isolated tracts of forest from 100 to 200 square miles in extent. This is the mountainous region of eastern Congo and western Uganda, which includes the 30-miles-wide Albertine rift, stretching from the Upper White Nile to the southern end of Lake Tanganyika. Two separate mountain massifs rise from the rift bottom: the Mountains of the Moon or Ruwenzoris where there are no gorillas, and south of them, on the borders between the Congo Republic and Rwanda, the chain of eight Virunga volcanoes, which form a dam across the rift to the north of Lake Kivu.

The eastern gorillas' habitat, which extends far up the slopes of the volcanoes, is one of extreme humidity, mist, cloud and heavy rainfall; and although day temperatures may be high, the nights are damp and cold. Indeed in 1926, during her stay of seven weeks in a camp at over 10,500 feet in the Virungas in November and December—the rainy season—Mary Akeley (widow of the American collector and naturalist Carl Akeley) recorded that day temperatures never rose higher than 46 degrees F. Moreover, with night temperatures falling to 32 or 34 degrees F, there was often hoar-frost at dawn, while during one three-day period hailstones carpeted the ground. When it was not raining there was dense mist, and the sun shone through briefly on only six occasions. Most of the steep mountain-sides of these central African volcanoes are girdled at altitudes of between 7,500 and 10,000 feet by almost pure stands of bamboo, 30 or 40 feet high, whose dense canopy of feathery plumes excludes almost all vegetation except small ferns, fine grasses and thick stands of wood-nettles, 6 to 8 feet tall. Although these nettles are virulent enough to sting through two layers of a man's clothing, the gorillas wade through them, incorporate them in their nests, and chew the stems and leaves, bristling with stinging hairs, with apparent immunity. Were it not for the gorillas themselves, and also buffalo and elephants breaking trails, the bamboo thickets would be negotiable only on all-fours. When the bamboo seeds, for the first and only time after many years' growth, it produces immense quantities of grain, which attracts plagues of forest rats but only a few small birds and the rather rare large francolins. And when the bamboo dies it becomes a skeletonal forest of spiky leaves and rotting stems, as thick as a man's thigh, shrouded in dank dripping mist. The dead canes creak and rattle together, and the wind moans through their hollow tops.

Above the bamboo at an altitude of 10,000 feet is the "cold forest," where large park-like glades are carpeted with kikuyu grass and an undergrowth of musk-thistles, goose-grass and wild celery, 6 or 8 feet tall. The parks are dominated by huge hagenia trees (often half reclining on the turf) 50 or 60 feet tall, with trunks 8 feet in diameter and massive branches flaring horizontally at near ground level and then soaring skywards to umbrella-shaped crowns, fashioned from clusters of long pinnate leaves. In March and April the hagenias blossom with a profusion of magenta flowers hanging like sprays of wistaria between the sparse foliage. The ocher-colored wood, from which the bark flakes raggedly, is not durable and many of the trees are hollow, providing homes for squirrels and other small animals. The many ancient trees among them are hung with clumps of parasitic ferns, cobwebs of *Usnea* lichens—the graybeard or Spanish moss—and trailing vines dotted with tiny yellow star-like flowers; while larger horizontal boughs are padded with thick cushions of dark green or golden-green moss, 2 or 3 feet wide and 20 or 30 feet long, from which the pink spikes of orchids spire. "Small hornless chameleons travel up and down and along their lower heavy branches [wrote Mary Akeley], or bask rigid and almost invisible in the tiny patches of golden sunshine that filter through the thick-growing leaves. Squirrels scurry to and fro, or sit chattering noisily on some mossy pedestal, decked with drooping fern fronds."

Between 10,000 and 11,500 feet the hagenia parkland gives way to giant tree-heaths more than 30 feet high and to forests of bushy rough-barked hypericums. The latter, the "wild rose," are 10 or 25 feet tall with very small lanceolate leaves and single bright-yellow flowers, and are festooned like the hagenias with beard lichens and mosses. Above the hypericum forest is the sub-alpine zone with its extensive clumps of blackberries, 10 to 12 feet high, which the gorillas eat when ripe though sour; and finally, between 11,000 and 14,000 feet, the alpine zone to which the gorillas sometimes climb. This is the fantasy world of giant senecios or tree-groundsels, 20 or 30 feet high and perhaps 200 years old, whose thick gnarled stems, ramifying like stag's horn coral, bear clusters of large ovate polished leaves at the apices of branches, and flowering heads more than a foot long; and of dense stands of giant lobelias on 6-foot stalks with clusters of long narrow leaves pointing skywards like candles, and with flowering spikes, like open fir cones, 7 or 8 feet long, covered with tiny purplish flowers that attract and are no doubt pollinated by brilliant green sunbirds. When gashed, the lobelia stalks exude a sticky and extremely bitter fluid that burns the eyes, though this does not deter gorillas from attempting to eat them.

There is not a great variety of wildlife in these mountain forests of the gorillas, though troops of from five to twenty or even sixty cat-sized golden monkeys with black crowns, shoulders and legs, visit the high forests to feed especially on the leaves and shoots of bamboo, and also on the galium vines and the blossom of vernonia shrubs. The commonest mammal is a large rufous-chestnut variety of the red forest duiker with horns only 3 inches long, though bush-pigs are present and elephants feed on the wild celery and raspberries and the seedling bamboos, 6 or 8 feet tall. Being expert climbers, the elephants also make their way up into the Budongo Forest in large numbers. In such swampy areas as Siba, from which there is easy access to grasslands outside the forest, herds of the large savanna buffalo are perhaps permanent residents, while the small forest buffalo graze in the glades of the sub-alpine zone, where leopards hunt the numerous tree hyraxes. Leopards, often very dark in color, are fairly common in the mountain forests and infrequently kill young and, exceptionally, adult male gorillas, as they do men. Peter Turnbull-Kemp has suggested that there may be a heavier concentration of leopards in the African rain-forest than anywhere else in their extensive Old World range, and that they may reach their maximum size in this habitat that contains few competitive predators in the form of lions or hunting dogs or men, but is well supplied with prey and also covert in which the cubs can be reared in the hollow trunks of fallen trees. But in fact we know very little about these forest leopards, though one suspects that they prey chiefly on small antelopes, monkeys and the larger rodents. However, a mysterious race of spotted lions has been reported so often from the Virungas that Leslie Brown suggests that not all these reports can refer to sub-adult true lions still retaining their cub spots. In 1937 a compatriot of mine at Cambridge, Kenneth Gandar-Dower, made an expedition to the Aberdare Mountains in search of these spotted lions; but although when tracking buffalo at an altitude above 12,000 feet he saw the spoor of a pair of lions, of which the female's was leopard-sized and the male's too small for a male lion, and also saw ordinary lions, he never succeeded in either seeing or shooting one. However, his more than ordinarily reliable native tracker, who had encountered these small lions on three or four occasions, described them as lightly built like cheetahs, with whiskers instead of proper manes, and spotted all over with rosettes; and a dressed skin from the Aberdares measures only 5 feet 10½ inches, excluding the 2-feet-9-inches tail, in comparison with the 9 feet 6 inches of a good-sized lion. The problem of the spotted lion remains to be solved.

Although the members of the eastern race of gorillas are

always referred to as mountain gorillas, three-quarters of them do not, according to George B. Schaller, live in the mountains, but below 5,000 feet in the hot and humid Congo basin. There, since there is little undergrowth on which to forage beneath the closed canopy of tall trees, they spend much of their time feeding in the more open lush valleys and along the rivers, whose clefts through the forest permit a luxuriant vegetation to thrive in the sunlight, though they retire at night to upper slopes and ridges. The Virunga volcanoes rise from one of the most densely populated and fertile regions of Africa; and the adjoining Albert (Kivu) National Park, 8,000 square miles in extent, was originally established in 1925 as a sanctuary for some of the mountain gorillas. Unfortunately, despite their shyness and although they avoid contact with the native inhabitants whenever possible, gorillas throughout the lower parts of their range are attracted to the plentiful sources of food provided by man's crops, fruit, trees and flowers, and return again and again to these, despite being speared and killed in considerable numbers at regular intervals in such areas as the Cameroons. A single small group of gorillas is capable of destroying half an acre of bananas or plantains in a couple of hours, though they do not in fact eat the fruit of either, but the pith of the stems which they chew and digest very thoroughly. The various groups of gorillas are not therefore spread evenly throughout their forest habitat, but tend to concentrate along roads in the vicinity of villages, especially where fields have gone out of cultivation but contain such favorite foods as ferns, the fruits and leaves of the musanga, the umbrella tree—so-called because of the sunshade shape of its shiny leaves—and various figs, especially the rough leaves of those known as the sandpaper leaf, because the natives use them for scouring their pots. Above all, gorillas like aframomum, as do most monkeys, and its mass of seeds, together with the sour pith within the tough green skin of the stem, forms 80 or 90 per cent of the lowland gorillas' total food.

Paradoxically, as Schaller has pointed out, the native African is both the enemy of gorillas, in that he kills them in order to protect his crops and in some regions hunts them for meat, and is also inadvertently their benefactor in that his primitive slash and burn type of shifting cultivation creates the "kaleidoscope patterns of forest regeneration" that provides them with their fa-

Gorilla

vorite foods. Since this method of cultivation is so important to gorillas it is worth quoting from Schaller's admirable description of the technique involved:

> With axe and fire they fell the forest trees, which then decay on the ground. After the smaller trees and shrubs have been burned, banana shoots are pushed into the ashes and shallow soil, and manioc may be planted beneath the bananas. . . . But . . . after three or four years the field is exhausted and must lie fallow for at least twelve years. . . . More forest is cleared and . . . villages are moved to be nearer the fields. . . .
>
> In the abandoned fields the new forest rises phoenix-like from the heart of the ashes . . . as the canopy becomes more and more continuous, less and less sunlight reaches the ground. . . . Many of the colonising plants cannot adapt themselves . . . the undegrowth disappears almost entirely. After about eighty years, tall forest again covers the ground where once villages and fields stood. The constant cutting, planting and abandoning have created a landscape consisting of ephemeral fields surrounded by a patchwork of forest in various stages of regeneration, and always on the horizon, the overpowering presence of the rain-forest.

Gorillas also tend to concentrate in the vicinity of such physical barriers as extensive areas of cultivation or grassland and especially broad rivers, for, like chimpanzees, they hesitate to enter even shallow pools, crossing streams, however narrow, only where fallen trees provide natural bridging; but even where there are no apparent physical barriers, isolated pockets of gorillas occur in the rain-forest. These are perhaps remnants of larger populations. For example, only 12 miles separate the dormant volcano of Mt. Mikeno in the Albert National Park, where gorillas are numerous, from the active Mt. Nyiragongo on which they have never been reported. Yet there is a continuous strip of forest, only a mile wide in one place, along the saddle between the two peaks, and elephants apparently pass to and fro. Possibly previous gorilla traffic was interrupted by volcanic eruptions, for in the 1920s sulphurous fumes killed most of the vegetation in the 10,000-feet zone.

That we know a great deal more about the eastern race of gorillas than we do of any members of the western race is due primarily to Schaller who undertook a ten months' study of them in the Virungas during 1959 and 1960, and more recently to another American, Dian Fossey, who watched other groups in the same region for more than 2,000 hours between 1967 and 1970 and is still watching them. Both set up camp at 10,000 feet in the "cold forest," and by literally living with them and winning their confidence by imitating their actions, the latter has established a relationship with individual gorillas as extraordinary as Jane Goodall's with chimpanzees; perhaps more extraordinary, if one takes into account the gorilla's shy nature and fearsome reputation. Regrettably, Dian Fossey has published rather little about her experiences, though we know that she was eventually able to approach to within a few feet of juveniles and subadults, who examined her knapsack and camera and even her bootlaces, and that one sub-adult male would actually touch her fingers and take fruit from the palm of her hand.

Contrary to popular belief, misled by the reactions of animals wounded by hunters, gorillas are, by and large, inoffensive and peaceful creatures and, so far as is known, resemble forest chimpanzees in probably never preying on other animals or eating carrion, though reputed to kill birds, rodents and small antelopes. In her long acquaintanceship with them Dian Fossey was threatened only once, when five males, believing her to be the cause of a juvenile member of their group falling out of a tree, charged but stopped when within 3 feet of her. Not that a threatening or displaying adult male gorilla, weighing between 378 and 504 pounds, is not a terrifying object to strike fear into the heart of the bravest man or girl when he repeatedly rears up on short bowed legs to his full height of 6 feet and whips up his massive arms to pound a rapid tattoo on his bare chest, striking alternately with cupped hands and producing a hollow *pok-pok-pok*. At the same time he gives vent to what Schaller has termed the most explosive sound in Nature: a single low-pitched but harsh roar, forced out through open mouth and audible at a distance of 3 miles. Roaring may be preceded by a number of hoots that gradually quicken until they merge into a continuous harsh growl. But if he has not been attacked or wounded, it is all magnificent bluff intended to intimidate both man and buffalo; and Schaller describes how his roars gradually become less frequent, and eventually he relaxes and reclines on the ground, propped up on his shaggy arms. His silky fur gleams with a blue-black sheen, and his black face shines as if polished beneath his brow-ridges and the hairy miter of his saggital crest. From time to time he reaches out lazily, with muscles of shoulders and broad back rippling, to pluck a leaf and stuff it into his cavernous mouth, whose large canines are coated with black tartar, while the other members of his group climb ponderously into shrubby trees and feed on the vines draped from the branches.

Schaller estimated the present population of gorillas in the Virunga forests at between 400 and 500: Dian Fossey put it at 375. This population is composed of numerous small groups, of which the largest on record included 43 members. Dian Fossey was able to identify 9 different groups with a total strength of 117 in her area of the Virungas, of which the smallest contained only 5 individuals and the largest 19, while Schaller's main study group comprised 21 individuals. Group numbers of lowland gorillas are very similar, averaging 16, with a maximum strength of 30. Schaller's main group consisted of 8 females with 5 infants, 3 juveniles (which are not weaned until they are nearly 3 years old), 1 sub-adult black-backed male and 4 adult silver-backed males, whose backs from shoulder-blades to rump are white by the time they have reached the age of 12, following the appearance of the first white hairs 2 or 3 years earlier. Dian Fossey's 9 groups included one of 5 males centered affectionately around a doddering old female of perhaps 50 years, until she died. All the males in these groups were very protective towards the infants and juveniles; and, significantly, there was much play among the younger members, once they were accustomed to the presence of a human being.

Each group of gorillas ranges continuously over 10 or 15 square miles of forest, but this nomadic feeding territory is not exclusive and may be visited from time to time by as many as six other groups. Two groups may even join forces and nest in company for a night (concentrating their sweet, musty odor), and the silver-backed leaders of the respective groups rarely fight, though one may put on a spectacular display, when two confront each other face to face and only an inch or two apart, hooting, beating his chest and leaping about; but bachelor groups, attempting to join up with "harem" groups, are not welcomed. Thus gorillas, like chimpanzees, are remarkable among mammals in their willingness to share, temporarily at any rate, their territory *and* its abundant food plants with other groups.

It is Dian Fossey's opinion that this coming together of various groups is responsible for more gorilla movement through the forests than seasonal changes in food sources. Nevertheless, certain foods attract concentrations of mountain gorillas as they do their lowland relatives. During one period of seven days in April one of Schaller's ten or eleven groups remained in an area about a mile long and half a mile wide, while meandering up into the bamboo zone and down into the forest, traversing a mile or so a day. Nearly half their food at this time consisted of young asparagus-like bamboo shoots which they shredded or peeled like bananas, discarding the tough hairy outer sheath and eating the tender white, bitter-sweet pith. The bamboo was supplemented by borage roots, the leaves of vines, and the juicy though bitter interior of wild celery, which in some districts is the gorillas' second staple food. Bamboo, however, covers only a small area of the mountain gorillas' habitat, and the shoots are seasonal. Abundant at the peak of the two rainy seasons from March to May and September to December, shoots are often totally absent during the dry seasons of January and February and from June to August. During the dry seasons the gorillas must therefore disperse in search of their thirty other mainly bitter food plants. Since these tend to be scarce in the bamboo forest, the hypericum zone is preferred, where the bark of young twigs is available and also the big cherry-like fruits of the pygeum, a large oak-like tree, though this bears fruit for only two or three months and is relatively scarce. Gorillas, like chimpanzees, rarely drink in the wild state, and there is indeed no permanent supply of water in some of their habitats.

The weight and massive build of gorillas prevent them from being truly arboreal, and the greater part of their daily life is spent on the ground, to which they also descend when alarmed. Though capable of walking bipedally for a distance of 20 yards they seldom do so for more than a few feet at a time, and normally progress quadrupedally in the manner of chimpanzees, supporting their heavy upper parts on the four fingers of their knuckles, with their hind-feet flat on the ground. Mature adults, though competent at climbing trees, do so only infrequently and slowly and deliberately, and are not good judges of whether or not branches will bear their weight. Indeed, when one of their favorite and very fattening foods, the rich oily fruits of the majap tree, ripens in October towards the end of the rainy season in the Cameroons, it is the juveniles and females, half the weight of the males, that climb for these, while the males must be content with those that are knocked down. Nevertheless, sleeping-nests are built both in the trees and on the ground, according to the suitability of the trees in a particular locality. It is difficult, for example, to construct a stable sleeping platform in a hagenia tree, the branches of which are brittle and snap. Gorillas bed down at dusk, between 5 and 6 o'clock, wherever they may happen to be feeding, though the juveniles, which may practice nest-building when only fifteen months old, rarely sleep apart from their mothers until they are nearly three years old. They do not stir again until the hour after sunrise, by which time they have had thirteen hours' sleep. Nevertheless, after a couple of hours' foraging they rest again from 9 or 10 o'clock until mid-afternoon, before feeding until dusk.

Dian Fossey's gorillas usually nested on the ground on crude beds of boughs, leaves, moss and loose soil; whereas when Schaller's main group remained in one locality for a week and used 106 nests, less than half were ground beds of bamboo, brush and vines, the remainder being either in the branches of trees or on the soft springy canopy of the bamboos. Ground nests may comprise no more than three or four handfuls of weeds packed down around the occupant to form a partial rim, on which he reclines on his belly, with his arms and legs tucked beneath him and his broad back presented to the drizzling rain. Merfield, however, describes an old male bedding down in an open glade where, among the secondary growth, there were plenty of canes and young saplings which he bent to the ground. Then, holding these down with his feet, he rotated, interlacing them until he had constructed a fine "spring mattress" capable of raising him above the damp earth. Finally, he stripped off the leafy tops of the saplings and laid these beneath him and around him until he was comfortably settled. Although tree nests are crudely put together in no more than half a minute or five minutes by bending and breaking surrounding twigs and branches, and involve none of the complex weaving and special manipulation of chimpanzees' or organgutans' nests, they provide reasonably stable platforms in forks or on horizontal limbs, from which their occupants will not fall off while asleep, when 15 or exceptionally 50 feet above the ground; and remain distinguishable as nests for a year or so. Unlike chimpanzees, gorillas do not make use of sticks as tools; they do not need to, since fruit and vegetable food is permanently to hand.

According to Schaller, gorillas have a high reproductive rate of perhaps 90 live births for every 1,000 head of their population (twice that of the highest human birth-rate), with a potential life-span of twenty or twenty-five years; but it is possible that half die before they reach maturity when between six and ten years old since they are susceptible to coughs and colds during periods of heavy rain, and also to yaws and a disease resembling leprosy. When their population has been reduced to a few thousand as in the case of the "mountain" gorillas, then they are clearly vulnerable to any external pressures on their habitat. Much of the food of those that live at lower altitudes depends, as we have seen, on the age-old slash and burn native agriculture. How will these lowland gorillas be affected by more modern methods of agriculture? We have also seen that the Albert National Park, and subsequently the Virungas, were originally intended as sanctuaries for the true mountain gorillas, and theoretically they are a protected species; but in practice, as Dian Fossey discovered at first hand, the boundaries of these sanctuaries are shrinking year by year. For instance, 25,000 acres of national park land have been appropriated for the cultivation of pyrethrum, resulting in the building of roads and settlements and the extermination of the wildlife. Ugandan and Rwandan poachers trap, hunt with bell-dogs, and kill throughout the park—not only animals but more than a score of extraordinarily devoted Congolese guards and wardens; groups of honey-collectors burn and hack down the hagenia trees; cattle range to every corner of the forests except the steepest mountain-sides and ravines, and their Batulsi herdsmen camp in the forests for months at a time undisturbed. The shy gorillas retreat ever further up the mountains and, in Dian Fossey's opinion, are doomed to extinction before the end of this century if present conditions prevail in the parks.

13: Doomed Orangutans: Successful Gibbons

We shall never know exactly how orangutans organized their society and their daily and seasonal routine in the years before massive destruction of their forest habitat in Borneo and northern Sumatra, together with the constant slaughter of females in order to procure their young for zoos, brought them to the verge of extinction. Ironically, they have no enemies except man and are, indeed, believed by the native Dayaks to be capable of killing both crocodiles and pythons. Because of the inaccessible nature of their forests no precise estimates of their present numbers can be made, but these are put at no more than between 450 and 700 in Sarawak and possibly 2,000 in North Borneo (Sabah), 1,000 in Indonesian Borneo and 1,000 in Sumatra—perhaps 4,500 in all. As an illustration of the inaccessibility of the orangutans' haunts, S. Dillon Ripley has noted that quite recently an experienced naturalist traveled rapidly for twenty-six days through one region of central Borneo without emerging into direct sunlight or encountering any place of past or present civilization. Their geographical distribution may have been restricted exclusively to Borneo and northern Sumatra at all times, though it has been suggested that climatic changes may have curtailed a much wider range throughout south-east Asia and its islands, and that they may have been exterminated in Java and Celebes during the Stone Age.

Today, the survivors inhabit only a fraction of their known range. The few hundred in Sarawak, for example, are scattered over 50,000 square miles, but actually occupy little more than 1/25 of this area, for their small impermanent groups of from two to six individuals are isolated in their forest blocks by human communication systems, by the ever-expanding population of the Dayaks and by rivers, since, like the other apes, they cannot swim and can only negotiate water barriers by natural bridges of fallen trees or tangles of lianas and creepers. So widely dispersed are these survivors that in 1964 Richard Davenport contacted no more than sixteen individuals, and these included only one group comprising male, female and infant, in the course of a seven-month intensive search for them in Sabah, despite the fact that he employed six native helpers equipped with walkie-talkies; and this was a greater number than any previous modern expedition had encountered. Although Davenport's quest coincided with the dry season when there was no fruit, and the orangs had scattered far and wide in their search for leaves and shoots, it seems probable that they are naturally solitary, for that superb Victorian naturalist, though ruthless collector, Alfred Russell Wallace, never saw two full-grown adults together; but there is no doubt that their population has drastically decreased and that it now includes an improportionate and adverse ratio of old and often isolated males, twenty or thirty years of age, to breeding females; though there would not appear to be any justification for suggesting that there were still several millions at the time of Wallace's travels. As a matter of fact his Dayak helpers were able to locate only twenty-one adults and juveniles and a number of young ones during his six months' stay in Borneo; and the Italian naturalist, Odoardo

Beccari, who arrived in Borneo a decade later than Wallace, collected only about thirty specimens during a stay of two and a half years in the late 1860s.

The orangutans' world is typical rain-forest with an upper canopy 120 or 150 feet above ground essentially lacking in undergrowth. Uniformly high temperatures and humidity prevail, and the annual rainfall amounts to 120 to 160 inches. But though the orangs range to an altitude of 3,000 feet and exceptionally to 6,000 feet, on isolated mountains on which the Dayaks have cultivated plantations, their main habitat lies below 500 feet in the swamp forests that border the major streams and the coast, and which stand in water a few inches or feet deep. Orangutans feed predominantly on fruit, mainly unripe and often very sour or bitter, though in the dry season when there is no fruit they take leaves, buds, orchids, ferns and mushrooms, and scrape behind loose bark and in rotten wood with their long, strong fingers for larvae and beetles. They also kill nestling birds and squirrels, and are reported to use sticks to open up bees' and ants' nests. In this respect a semi-wild young male, belonging to Barbara Harrisson of the Sarawak Museum, picked up a stick from the forest floor and chased and hit a snake before it could escape down a hole, though its companion, a young female, fell out of her tree at the shock of seeing the snake. But orangutans probably handle sticks and branches mainly in intimidation displays and in frustration, though a male, one of whose arms Wallace had broken with a rifle-ball, broke off substantial branches with which to fashion a nest that concealed him from the men below. Another male, after fleeing from George Schaller for three-quarters of an hour, finally stopped and broke off a dry branch with the palm of his hand and watched it crash to the ground; and during the next half hour or so bent numbers of branches until they snapped and then hurled them down. Similarly, a female with a large infant threw down about thirty branches, varying in size from twigs to limbs 10 feet long and 3 inches in diameter, in the course of a quarter of an hour, expending considerable effort in wrenching off the latter. Some of these were allowed to fall from her side, but in other instances she would look down at Schaller, while swinging a branch like a large pendulum and, at the peak of the arc closest to him, release it; or, alternatively, lift a branch as high as her chest or above her head with one hand, and hurl it down forcefully. Schaller commented that: "Whatever interpretation is given this behaviour, there is no doubt that it induced me to jump nimbly at times, and that it kept me effectively away from beneath the tree." Wallace also had similar experiences with four females. Three of these he had wounded, while the fourth, who was feeding on the unripe fruits of a durian tree (in the company of several young beasts), began breaking off branches and the large spiny fruits with every appearance of rage, as soon as she saw him, "causing such a shower of missiles as effectually kept us from approaching too near the tree."

The daily and seasonal activities of orangutans, and no doubt the social structure of their groups, must have been ordered, as in the case of chimpanzees, by the sporadic ripening of the various fruits over a wide area, and also perhaps by their craving for a particular fruit, with families or groups covering extensive feeding territories, and settling in one locality for several days only when fruit was abundant. According to Barbara Harrisson, females with nursing young are often hard-put to find sufficient food and are obliged to travel long distances in search of it, thereby exposing themselves to the danger of coming into contact with the Dayaks who also like orangutan fruits. She suggests, too, that it is some years before a young orang becomes fully acquainted with the geography of its group's extensive range, since it is wholly dependent on its mother for food and protection for the first six months or longer; and like the young chimpanzees, continues to follow her until perhaps four or five years old, when it joins a small "teenage" group until maturing at the age of ten.

A fruit much sought after by orangutans is that of the 100-foot, sparsely foliaged and difficult to climb durian tree, of which a square mile of forest may contain only a single specimen. Durian fruits are eaten by many jungle animals, including tigers and also elephants which swallow them whole. They ripen from pale green to a golden yellow at the peak of each monsoon and, according to the natives of Sumatra, this is the one occasion when groups of orangutans congregate—or used to—in a single locality, attracted no doubt by the fruits' powerful odor. Barbara Harrisson was present one morning, when two orangs, who had kept warm during a rainy night by sleeping in the same nest, began the day's activities. At 6:45 A.M. they climbed slowly across to a durian tree and bit off the stems of the fruits from a branch. Then, supporting the football-sized fruits weighing 5 or 6 pounds from below with one hand, they wrenched open the thick, very tough outer skins, sharply studded with close-set conical spines, tearing and splitting them with teeth and hands, and plunged their heads deep inside to the soft cream-colored, custard-like pulp, which opens into sections like an orange. After this early feed they rested in the nest from 8 A.M. to 10 A.M. before resuming their activities, when one broke off the whole crown of a young tree and ate the leaves while hanging by one arm from a branch. The flesh of a durian is juicy and of a delicious flavor even to a man, if its appalling stench—compounded of rotten eggs, onions and putrid meat—is ignored, and Wallace described it as a rich butter-like custard highly flavored with almonds, and worth a voyage to the East to experience; but it is possible that orangs eat only the eight to fifteen chestnut-sized seeds within the pulp, for a female (with a small infant) watched by Schaller discarded the pulp but ate the seeds of at least fifteen fruits, wasting only half of one seed; and Wallace also refers to their partiality to seeds.

Although male orangutans weigh 154 to 168 pounds when full-grown, and females half as much, they stand little more than 4 feet high, and their very long and powerful arms, spanning more than 7 feet, and short strong legs, with feet almost the equivalent of a second pair of hands, fit them well for a wholly arboreal existence. They rarely need to descend to the ground, and do not do so to retrieve any fruit they drop; but when tree foods are scarce they may come down to eat the shoots and fruits of a small palm (*Zalacca conferta*). Similarly, in very dry weather they drink from streams or river banks, either directly with their mouths or by cautiously wetting their hands and then sucking them, and they also fling water over their faces; but in the normal course of events they obtain water from tree hollows or the bulbs of water-storing epiphytes, by sipping dew on mosses or orchids, or by sucking raindrops off their hairy arms. The grasping power of the orangutans' feet enables them to hang with ease in almost any position, and to obtain fruit while hanging by one hand and foot. Barbara Harrisson watched one—clad in a shaggy, dark chestnut-red coat of long fur, that fell smoothly from the crown of his head to his legs—standing on a twisted branch, while holding on to a vine with one hand and scraping away industriously with his other at the bark, poking a finger into it and peeling it with his teeth. Although orangs can travel through the trees faster than a man can make his way over the forest floor, they climb with considerable care, always grasping as many branches as possible, and do not normally brachiate for more than 3 or 4 yards at a time. Along horizontal boughs

Orangutan

they progress quadrupedally and, when transferring from one tree to another, either reach for and secure a firm hold on the foliage of the adjoining tree before swinging over the gap, or inch out on to a small horizontal limb until this bends beneath their weight and brings them within grasping distance of another branch; but only when its hands are anchored securely to the latter does an orang release its feet-hold on the first branch.

Orangutans, like chimpanzees, usually construct new nests or sleeping platforms every night. These can be constructed in five or six minutes, or even in not much more than a minute. But they use the same nests when resident for several days in a locality well supplied with fruit, when sick, when a female is giving birth, or during prolonged periods of heavy rain. Although an orang's thick fur is rain-proof, it may in these conditions build a shelter resembling a normal sleeping-nest, but works at its construction from below instead of from above. Nests are usually sited at heights of between 30 and 80 feet; but they may be placed almost anywhere in a tree, providing that a supporting foundation is available, together with an adequate supply of small branches with which to construct a stable platform, and most nests have a lining of 12-inch twigs, though few of these are completely detached. Barbara Harrisson has described how one large male constructed his nest. Walking along a high branch with a bough between his teeth, he stepped into the nest feet first, while holding on to a branch that projected from the nest like the handle of a frying-pan. Then taking hold of the bough with both hands, he raised it above his head for a second, before placing it inside the nest, with the leaves at the tip of the bough innermost, subsequently standing on top of it and padding it down firmly with his fists. Then he left the nest again, to return after two or three minutes with a large durian fruit dangling by its stem from his teeth; but after placing the fruit on the nest, he went off in search of another branch, which he folded underfoot in the nest, and then sat down. Bending forward, he began to pick at loose bits of leaves sticking out from the sides of the nest and from below the platform, snipping them off with his fingers and placing them beneath and around his body, while pivoting slowly. By this time, after a quarter of an hour's fiddling, it was dusk, and he finally lay back, though still grasping the nest "handle" with one hand, while with the other he scratched and adjusted a branch once more: "We sat still for a long time, while the forest grew dark and the mosquitoes danced around us with their irritating high-pitched hum. . . . There was no more movement."

During the dry season in Sabah, with its associated scarcity of fruit, Richard Davenport noted that 90 per cent of the orangutans under observation were not stirring from their nests in the morning until 7:45 A.M.—one did not rise until after midday!— and were settled in their nests again by 6:30 P.M., despite having spent considerably more than half of the intervening hours resting or napping. Barbara Harrisson camped out one night in order to watch an orang awaken to a new day. At dawn:

> I saw a dark body, back turned slightly upwards under a covering of twigs, feet folded under the belly. One hand was tucked under the shoulder, the other gripped a branch that stuck out from the roof of foliage, smoothing away the wetness of the night. Leaves, orchids, vines and ferns exhaled a faint mist that floated upwards. . . . A delightful spectacle followed, the Grande-Levée of jungle-man. He sat up, looked about, scratching his back. He lifted his elbows sideways, first rubbing the eyes; inhaled deeply, stretched his back straight and flung out wide, first one fist, then the other, to each side. Slumped back, exhaling. Sat, to look down over the edge of the nest. He scratched his back between the shoulder-

blades, slowly but firmly, again and again. He stretched once more, this time bending and straightening his legs; sat for a while gazing. . . . Then he started to poke round inside his nest.

In view of the decline in their population it seems unlikely that many more such descriptions of orangutan life will be penned. By contrast, tens or possibly hundreds of thousands of gibbons still range over south-east Asia from Assam to Burma, Thailand, Indo-China, Hainan, Malaya, Sumatra and Borneo, inhabiting both tropical rain-forest and the partially deciduous monsoon forests. Since their habitats extend from sea-level to above 7,000 feet, where temperatures can fall to freezing point, they have clearly been able to adapt themselves to a wide range of climatic conditions and foods, though our knowledge of the life-histories of the half-dozen or dozen species of gibbons is very sketchy. They are predominantly inhabitants of the middle layers of the forest, though ascending into the canopy for fruit and descending to the ground to hunt insects and to eat the brackish soil near springs. Although gibbons, like apes, have no tails which, in the case of the spider monkeys serve as a fifth or, rather, a first hand, they are the supreme exponents of brachiation. Since gibbons weigh only 12 or 20 pounds and since their arms, which reach down to their ankles, are so muscular that a captive gibbon can pull a 154-pound man up to the bars of its cage, they are both light enough and strong enough to "fly" through the forest, brachiating hand over hand, 20 or 30 feet at a time, in long-armed swings from branch to branch. The slightest touch on a branch enables them to change direction in mid-flight, rebounding 40 or 50 feet over a clearing or narrow stream—they cannot swim—to another tree, though they also take full advantage of the vines strung from tree to tree and hanging from them in cables. Ripley has described their descent in a matter of seconds from the topmost branches to the ground as a breath-taking series of controlled falls and huge leaps in "a bewildering cascade of bouncing forms and shaking branches, accompanied by loud whoops startling to the ear." Such is their agility that they can actually capture birds in flight. Nevertheless, gibbons, like the less aerial chimpanzees, are accident prone, for an examination of 233 skeletons of the white-handed or lar gibbon revealed that more than a quarter of the mature animals and half of the older adults had suffered fractured bones.

More than three-quarters of the gibbons' food consists of fruits, mainly bitter and sour—mangoes, blue plums, grapes and especially various kinds of figs and the bamoo, whose fruity, fibrous meat and ten or twelve seeds is contained in a tough avocado-like shell; but leaves, buds, flowers, lizards, squirrels, nestling birds and grasshoppers are also eaten, and ants are licked off the backs of their hands, while water is obtained by licking dew or raindrops from leaves or bark, or by dipping their hands in water, while hanging from a branch, and sucking the drops from hair and knuckles.

Most gibbons live in family parties of from two to six members, though in some species an adult male may lead a loosely knit group of fifteen to twenty followers. Although classified as apes and not monkeys, the gibbons' social structure and territorial behavior resemble those of the howler monkeys, since each family party or troop occupies a territory of from 35 to 300 acres, the retention of which is associated with a vocal display; and, unlike other apes, they do not build sleeping-nests, though they roost in certain favorite trees whose rather dense crowns provide shelter. Most of our knowledge of the common gibbons' life-history stems from Clarence May Carpenter's study of them in a mountainous region of northern Thailand in the 1930s. Ac-

cording to his account these gibbons begin to stir in their roost-
ing-trees at dawn, and shortly after doing so begin their morning serenade. This is taken up by groups in adjacent territories,
until all have serenaded repeatedly during the hour after dawn.
Only then do the various groups set out leisurely on the day's
search for food. However, in the course of its travels one group
may draw near to another, and this encounter incites the
members of both groups to vocal protest. If this does not result
in one or other group retreating, or if both want to feed on the
same fruit tree or to follow the same route through the jungle,
then a more intensive vocal "battle" ensues, during which the
members of each group call loudly and frequently, with the
males hooting and the females' series of whoops rising to a
shrieking crescendo, until one group finally does retreat.

Although Carpenter interpreted these territorial battles purely
in terms of the vocal superiority or sonority of one group over
another, it is arguable that the associated chimpanzee-like
branch shaking, together with the sallies and chases of individuals, are actually more effective in the retention of territories.
However, the largest of the gibbons, the siamangs, which are
less agile than other gibbons perhaps because they have less
scope for acrobatics in the dense canopy of south-western Sumatra's foggy rain-forest, also employ vocal territorial displays,
booming and bellowing and modulating their calls by slapping
their mouths lightly with cupped hands. A German zoologist,
Emil Selenka, has described how every morning the troops of
siamangs filled forest and valley with their song:

Usually the song only began around nine o'clock as soon as
the sun had broken through the regular morning fog cover. A
few old males started the song by emitting very deep bell-like
sounds and then females and younger animals joined in with a
resounding, high, jubilant shout which was followed by a

deafening high laugher. This forest music, which is audible for the distance of an hour's walk, slowly falls into increasingly softer tones.

Since gibbons are meticulous feeders, peeling or shelling their fruit, removing the seeds, and chewing the pulp very thoroughly, they are slow eaters, and their morning feed lasts for about two hours. This is followed by a three-hour interval for rest, grooming and play in a tree sheltered from the sun and strong winds. The afternoon feeding session is less intensive, and if this is interrupted by a shower, each animal sits hunched up until the rain stops, when intensive grooming precedes their next move. In the evening the gibbons travel back to a suitable roosting-tree, where there is a period of mild activity before they settle down for the night at or a little before sunset, and once again a chorus of rising and falling hoots spreads through the forest.

14: Animal Relationships in Asian Jungles

There are two major groups of monkeys in Asian forests, the macaques and the langurs or leaf monkeys. Troops of from ten to thirty aggressive macaques mainly inhabit the middle and ground storeys of the forest, whereas the less aggressive langurs keep to the storey above the macaques when both are present in the same forest, and often climb into the upper canopy. Langurs do not possess cheek pouches in which to store food, like the omnivorous macaques and baboons, but chew their leaf food very thoroughly and then digest it with the aid of bacteria in their triple-chambered stomachs. Since they appear to pass much of the day sitting in the treetops and also, like lemurs, bask in the early morning and late evening sun, it has been suggested that langurs are less active than other monkeys because of the long period of digestion required to extract the maximum nourishment from their not very nutritious leaf diet; but they eat fruit too, while the African colobuses, which are also leaf eaters, are very active monkeys.

In Asia true rain-forest is extensive from Malaya south to Sumatra and Borneo, but occurs only in relatively small patches on the mainland, in India, Burma and Thailand. The typical forest of much of India, where a wet season is followed by a rainless season, is monsoon forest, which, although always including some trees in leaf, is predominantly leafless and barren during the dry months, and burgeons with the rains. The existence of close ecological and protective relationships between different kinds of mammals, and between mammals and birds, is particularly obvious in these more open forests with grassy clearings of India. When, for example, langurs are feeding in a tree, a crowd of the beautiful white-spotted chital deer often wait beneath it, for these monkeys tend to feed selectively, taking only the stalk of a leaf or one bite out of a fruit and then dropping the other parts, which are immediately eaten up by the waiting deer. On one occasion George Schaller observed a group of chital to wait around a fig tree for ten hours until its langur occupants finally left it; and on another occasion, when a langur came down from a tree with a leafy branch, a chital buck actually began to nibble at the leaves in the monkey's hands, before the latter jerked the branch aside and retreated to the top of a termites' mound where it could eat undisturbed.

Both monkeys and birds are invaluable allies of deer and antelope in warning them of the approach of such predators as tigers and leopards: "The flushing of a jungle fowl, the screechings of jungle babblers and red-wattled lapwings, the calling of a langur . . . are immediately investigated," remarks Schaller. "On several occasions a herd became aware of the proximity of a tiger only after having responded to the sharp *ka-koa-ka* of an alarmed langur." During the hours of daylight a troop of langurs will keep a prowling tiger or leopard under continuous observation, uttering their hoarse, coughing alarm calls for as long as the predator is in sight; and this alarm is taken up by one troop after another over a distance of three miles. Nevertheless, langurs are often the prey of both leopards and tigers, which, like jaguars, are partial to monkey meat. At night, the mere presence of a leopard or tiger beneath the roosting-tree of a troop of black-faced langurs or hanumans is sufficient to induce hysteria among them. Initially this takes the form of extreme excitement, in which they leap from branch to branch, shrieking and shaking the foliage, while excreting showers of droppings. Then, as their hysteria increases, they scramble frantically around the crown of the tree in crazy circles until finally one, exhausted and unable to control its movements, crashes to the ground. Others may crash down after it and lie motionless as if in a state of hypnosis, though should the leopard or tiger be shot at this stage, the monkeys slowly come to their senses and ultimately move off.

Subjected to the langurs' continual abuse, a tiger snarls and bares its fangs, and may charge with a series of terrifying roars and growls at their tree and even leap up into its lowest fork. This frightening demonstration so unnerves the monkeys that instead of retreating to or remaining in the upper branches, where they would be safe from the most agile young tiger, they panic and either fall while attempting to swing across too wide a gap or, inexplicably, descend and make a futile effort to cross 20 yards of open ground to another tree. Tigers are more proficient climbers than generally credited, capable of springing to a height of 13 feet when "servicing" their talons on soft-barked trees, while a young light-weight tiger can swarm up a 60-foot tree devoid of branches for the first 45 feet.

There is a close and constant association between deer and birds. Schaller watched a peacock courting an unreceptive chital with the full panoply of its gorgeous display, while "mynah birds readily perched on the backs of chital and appeared to search for ectoparasites; black drongos sat on their heads and snapped insects flushed by their hooves; and jungle crows pulled strips of velvet from the antlers of the bucks." But there is no closer association than that between the great gaur—the seladang of Malaya and Indo-China—and those wariest of birds, the large-bantam jungle fowl, which range through Asia from Kashmir to Singapore, nesting in clumps of bamboo, and are the ancestors of all the world's poultry. Gaur and their rather smaller relatives, the banteng, are the largest and also the most beautiful of all cattle. Standing 6 or 7 feet at the withers and weighing upwards of a ton, a bull gaur is jet-black or dark chestnut with black-pointed, golden horns measuring 3 or 4 feet along their outside span, while cows and young beasts are a glowing brown, and newborn calves red, bay or light-chestnut; and all are distinguished by long golden-white stockings, reaching from their hooves to just above their hocks, as if they had walked through wet sand. Charles Ogilvie, a former superintendent of Malaya's King George V Park, has described how he often watched jungle fowl darting about under the bellies of grazing seladang when catching the grasshoppers they disturbed. One herd of seven seladang was accompanied by eight jungle fowl, comprising three adult cocks, four adult hens and a well-grown cockerel which operated for several minutes on a gaping wound at the base of the right horn of one of the cows, removing dead tissue and a score of maggots. Throughout the operation the cow never moved, winced or opened an eye. Ten days later, when Ogilvie was watching the herd again, the cow was lying down ruminating; but, on the cockerel approaching, she stretched out her head along the ground and tilted her horn so that the cockerel might clean up the wound.

As jungle fowl take advantage of insects flushed by the grazing seladang, so wood partridges are provided with some of their food by the bearded boars of Malaya and Borneo. Since acorns are too bulky for these partridges to swallow whole they accompany feeding pigs and, when the latter are crunching acorns, crowd about them, picking up the fallen morsels and even pecking them from a boar's lips. This favor they repay by cackling their alarum if any predator approaches.

Although small herds of seladang and sambar deer may graze in the same open glassy glade or maidan in a Malayan forest, they do not actually intermingle, as do the various species of deer and antelope and also pig. Nevertheless, the wary sambar warns the seladang of the presence of a tiger, and there are a number of records of a close relationship developing between a solitary sambar stag and a bull seladang that has been deposed from the leadership of the herd; such an association, with the stag acting as a kind of watchdog companion, may continue for several years. In contrast to chital and barasingha (swamp deer) which are predominantly grazers, sambar are predominantly forest deer, occasionally venturing out into the maidans at dusk and during the night, but retreating into the forest again an hour before dawn; and the fact that they are both grazers and browsers, feeding during the hot season, when grasses shrivel up, on the universally popular fruits of figs and tamarinds, whose long brown velvety pods contain many large acid seeds relished by birds and monkeys and also wild pig, accounts for their wide distribution throughout a variety of habitats in Asia.

The gaur are also grazers of grass and browsers of bamboo shoots, leaves, shrubs and fruits, and are reputed to be mainly nocturnal, lying up in the hill forests by day and grazing on the maidans at dawn and in the late evening or, in some regions, visiting the maidans only during the hot season when the foliage has been burnt and the streams have run dry and the flies have become intolerable in the forest. But whether an animal is nocturnal or diurnal so often depends upon the degree of disturbance to which it is subjected by man. In Java, for example, banteng graze on the maidans at all hours of the day, and even under a blazing sun, where not disturbed.

But the jungle animal who comes into contact with almost every other animal, and around whom evolves so much of Asian forest life is—or was—the tiger. Was, alas, because even in the ten years since I published what I tried to make an objective account of the tiger's life-history, and was taken to task for suggesting that by the end of this century the only wild tigers would be those in national parks, their extermination has in fact proceeded faster than I had feared. Today, less than 2,000 remain in India and perhaps as many more in Malaya, together with an unknown but obviously decreasing number in Thailand and Indo-China. This tale of decreasing populations applies of course to many other animals in Asia and elsewhere, and any account of wildlife must to some extent be past history.

An interesting study in itself would be the influence of ecological factors on the seasonal routine of tigers. Deer and antelope, for example, are particularly partial to the acid orange fruits of the bher thornbush, and so long as this bush is bearing fruit, tigers are never very far away from the game it attracts. The oak-like mhowa tree, which blooms so profusely that a single tree may carry a hundredweight or more of fleshy flowers, is similarly attractive. When the flowers fall in March or April their heavily scented and intoxicating petals draw not only families of sloth bears, but chital and sambar deer, nilghai antelope and indeed most mammals and also birds, and the predatory tigers. On the other hand when millions of caterpillars are defoliating large blocks of teak woods, the jungle is bared to sun and hot winds that scorch up the undergrowth; deprived of shade and covert, both game and tigers must emigrate elsewhere.

Sloth bears are particularly addicted to the mhowa blossoms, and also to the similarly fleshy flowers of the senna, and a single hour of moonlight may bring a succession of as many as seven

Sloth bear

bears to visit one mhowa tree after another. Fruit and insects form the bulk of the sloth bears' food, and when such trees as figs, ebony, jujube, jaman and the aromatic bel are fruiting in the hot season, regular rounds are made of these, and the fruit either shaken down or climbed for. All tropical bears climb well, aided by sharp claws and the rough skin on the naked soles of their curved feet, and a sloth bear can swarm up the smoothest bole into the topmost branches of a pallu tree in order to obtain its sweet sticky fruit. After the heavy monsoon rains the bears raid the ripening crops of sugar-cane and maize, and if villagers are tapping date-palms climb thcse to drink the toddy from the catching-pots. They also rifle the small forest bees' combs in hollow trees and the large rock bees' huge combs which hang in clusters from the branches of trees or the undersides of rocks.

During the monsoon there is an abundant supply of insects and grubs in bark crevices and under stones and logs, and a sloth bear can scent a grub under 3 feet of earth, and dig down with remarkable rapidity to the galleries of the large white larvae of dung-beetles and longicorns. But most sought after by both sloth bears and sun bears are termites. The former's method of extracting termites is both efficient and amusing to watch. After breaking open or burrowing into a termitary with his 4-inch-long, ivory-white claws, he gets down to it, with rump elevated, and first blows away with prodigious huffs and puffs the finer layers of dust resulting from his excavations, before siphoning out the termites and larvae from their galleries. This is evidently an exhausting operation, for his flanks heave and from time to time he draws back for air. His powers of suction are increased by such physical peculiarities as a hollowed palate and the absence of the middle pair of incisors in his upper jaw permitting the passage of air through the gap. His mouth therefore works as a vacuum cleaner; the nozzle or muzzle is hairless, the lips protrusible, and the snout mobile, while the nostrils can be closed at will.

Sloth bears live in a favorable habitat of dense jungle in which food is plentiful all the year round. There is probably no necessity for tropical bears ever to venture further out of their jungles than the marginal plantations, and there is no evidence that sloth bears or sun bears ever migrate, though the former's habitat includes the wooded foothills of the Himalayas and the latter lives as high as 5,000 feet in Borneo. However, sloth bears, like tigers, are dependent on a constant water supply. Their first act on emerging from their lairs in the evening is to drink, and if their regular source of water fails they must either dig for it in the dried-up bed of a stream or travel many miles to another water-hole. This dependence on water makes it all the stranger that in Ceylon they inhabit only the driest regions of the low country, never frequenting the wet jungle zone nor, for that matter, the hills. In Ceylon they forage at any time of the day during cool wet weather, and in these conditions in India usually sleep in tall grass or under a tree or in a shady thicket or clump of bamboo; but during the hot season, though well insulated by a thick shaggy coat of coarse hair, which falls like a cape over neck and shoulders, and more tolerant of the sun's heat than such jungle inhabitants as tigers, they prefer caves or hollow trees in which the temperature remains constant, and in which they are sheltered from heavy rain and can gain relief from the plagues of flies. From dawn until shortly before sunset the sloth bear idles away the hours in his cave, buzzing and humming while licking his paws. Why do bears, and especially sloth bears and sun bears, spend so much time sucking their paws? Do they do so because much of their food is sticky or juicy or because there may be a sticky secretion between their pads, or merely as the ursine equivalent of "doodling"?

Tropical bears do not require permanent retreats or dens, for though sloth bear cubs usually appear in August or September in Ceylon, there is no definite breeding season, and the one or two (rarely three) cubs can be born in any dry cave or "earth" in a bank, while a hollow log or a tree platform suffices for a sun bear's cubs. The cubs only require shelter from heavy rain or excessive heat for a short period after birth, and a sloth bear's cubs are accompanying her on foraging expeditions when three weeks old, climbing on to her back if threatened by any predator. Appreciable numbers of bears must be killed by tigers, whether sloth bears in jungles, black bears in the Himalayan foothills or brown bears in the Manchurian cedar forests, though a large sloth bear, weighing 200 or 300 pounds, is capable of inflicting fearful injuries with its 4-inch claws, and a black bear can vanquish a tiger if not actually kill it.

Tigers inhabit, or recently inhabited, an extraordinary variety of habitats. These range from their strange saline swamp environment in the Sunderbans, described in *Life at the Sea's Frontiers*, a previous volume in this series, to the montane cedar-forests of Manchuria. There are tigers in the rain-jungles of Indonesia and Malaya, where it is twilight at midday beneath the dense canopy, and in Assam's almost impenetrable jungles of teak, ironwood and silk-cotton trees. There are tigers in the Terai, where dense wet jungle alternates with vast swampy areas. The Terai adjoins the Nepalese foothills of the Himalayas, with their spacious savannas of feathery-tipped elephant grass 8 or 10 feet high, 20 feet in places. Here and there a great tree rears its lofty crown above this grass-jungle, through whose tangle of stems almost as thick as bamboo even elephants and rhino have difficulty in forcing a passage. Still denser belts of 20-foot reeds conceal numerous *gheels*, on the marshy edges of which tigers lie up in hot weather. But after the savannas have been burnt by villagers and herdsmen, the resulting park-like grassy maidans become the favorite grazings of large numbers of deer and wild pig and thousands of domestic cattle, with their attendant tigers. Moreover the lower reaches of the numerous rivers that flow down from the Himalayas and meander through the Terai are studded with islands, each a jungle in its own right of elephant-grass, tamarisk and stands of gigantic sal and shisham trees. Their matted undergrowth of brake and creepers forms ideal covert for tigers, which can retreat when hunted to the deep gorges of the foothills above.

Tiger country must fulfil three conditions. First, it must contain adequate stocks of deer or wild pig, or cattle and other domestic stock in nearby villages, for the average tiger consumes between 4,000 and 5,500 pounds of meat a year, representing half as much again liveweight in the form of, say, thirty sizeable deer; second, abundant supplies of water; and third, extensive covert in which to lair and also to lie up during the heat of the day, though in the shady Indian sal forests or the sunlit teak and mixed woods of Burma and Assam tigers are on the move at all hours in the cool season. That tigers prospered in hot countries and built up populations running into hundreds of thousands is not to be attributed primarily to favorable climatic conditions, but to the abundant game, water and heavy covert provided by their forests and dense grass jungles and reed beds. Tigers are indeed as notable for their intolerance of the direct rays of the tropical sun as they are for their liking for reed beds, pools and streams: whereas leopards are tolerant of the sun and are not distressed by the lack of water.

Although Indian forests are not, in the main, as dense as the rain-jungles of south-east Asia, west Africa and South America, grazing for deer and other game is largely restricted to the grassy maidans and to the scrub and forest edges, and their herds are usually broken up into much smaller aggregations than those inhabiting the savanna type of country. It is not therefore practical for tigers to hunt in prides as lions do, and every tiger usually works his own hunting territory, which may be a roughly triangular block of jungle with points 5 or 8 miles apart or have a circumference of 100 miles. If he makes a kill, he remains near it for two or three days, if not disturbed, before continuing on his regular round, which he is likely to cover every five or ten days. Although as many as a dozen tigers may share a jungle block of 20 or 30 square miles in the remoter parts of Assam, concentrations of tigers normally only occur when their hunting territories are contracted by fire or drought or, especially in Indo-China, by floods, when large numbers of game flock to or are stranded on small islands, and provide the local tigers with temporary bonanzas. It follows then, that with only sufficient prey in each territory for a single tiger or tigress and cubs, the latter are eventually evicted, usually when about two and a half years old, to seek their own unoccupied jungle blocks. But suitable jungles are usually already occupied by adult tigers, since there is a curious tendency for the vacant territory of a dead tiger to be filled by another tiger, and that of a tigress by another tigress, and the young tigers must make do with less favorable jungles.

Seasonal weather changes and plagues of insects are also responsible for tiger movement. Mass migrations from the forests to the dry uplands of Manchuria occur in bad summers when the swarms of mosquitoes resemble the smoke from forest fires; while in Indo-China tigers retreat deep into the jungles during the hot season, but during the rainy season from June to September roam through the hill pine forests, which are frequented by sambar, muntjac and hog-deer, by wild pig, and by buffalo and gaur. In India, any inclination to migrate long distances during the hot season, which extends from March to the onset of the monsoon towards the end of June, is restricted by the paramount necessity of remaining in the vicinity of the few waterholes that have not dried up, with shade temperatures of 110 degrees F by day and only 10 or 14 degrees lower at night; but with the coming of the monsoon rains the game disperse, and the tigers follow them within a radius of 15 to 20 miles from their headquarters.

The first tigers to colonize the prey-full jungles of Asia, very possibly as immigrants from Siberia, must have been game killers. Only when the jungles had become saturated with their own kind, and when the expanding human population began to make inroads into the jungles, did they become cattle killers and, to a very small extent—except under abnormal conditions in certain districts—man killers. And everywhere their main prey has been wild pigs which, being nocturnal, invariably near water, and herding in sounders of ten or twenty or more sows and piglets, are easy prey for tigers; yet, paradoxically, the boar is one of the few animals in the jungle that is not only a match for tigers and totally fearless of them, but will actually attack one without provocation. Equipped with razor-sharp tusks 7 to 13 inches in length, protected by a shield of cartilage ¾ inch thick over the shoulders, and reaching weights of 200 or 300 pounds or, reputedly, 600 pounds (considerably more than the average tiger) in Manchuria, a boar will share a jungle path with a tiger, drink at a water-hole when flanked on either side at a discreet distance by a leopard and a tiger, or trot unchallenged through a ring of four leopards. Although adult tigers are extremely wary of attacking boars that they cannot take by surprise, many inexperienced young tigers have been disemboweled by the long clean rips of their tusks.

In Indonesia there are crested pigs with prominent manes, and in Malaya bearded pigs distinguished by heavy growths of curly white whiskers around the huge wart-like and bristle-covered growths on their snouts. These Asian pigs, like those of Africa, have many fascinating habits. In cold or wet weather the boars, and no doubt the sows too, sleep on beds of small branches laid neatly side-by-side in tunnel-like shelters, which they form by biting off bunches and branches of leaves; and the boars assist the sows to construct farrowing "arbors" in the dense undergrowth in which the piglets remain for perhaps a couple of weeks after birth, since all newborn piglets are very sensitive to falls in temperature. These shelters are basically heaps of grass, ferns and small branches, 3 feet high and 6 or 9 feet wide, lined with dry palm leaves, and with a well-concealed entrance at the base.

Every few years both bearded and crested pigs undertake mass dispersals from coastal areas into the hills. In Indonesia these apparently coincide with the beginning of the rainy season, and in Malaya with the drying out of the coastal swamps. Although these migrations are reported to operate irrespective of whether food is scarce or plentiful in the coastlands, the naturalist E. Banks believed that in Borneo they were linked to the slightly irregular, seven-year fruiting cycle of some forest trees. In Borneo the bearded pigs are normally scattered in ones and twos in fairly well-defined areas from seashore and river marge in particular to mountain tops; but an irruption of fruit attracts alien populations for a few weeks, whose numbers churn up the forest floor into the likeness of a ploughed field, before they move out when the fruiting season ends. These invasions occasionally assume the proportions of mass migrations, and twice in twenty years Banks witnessed such movements, which continued for as long as a month, when herds of pigs were traveling purposefully, directly and silently through the jungle and across rivers in convoys of thirty or forty. In all regions these migrations result in a large-scale slaughter of the participants by both men and (in Malaya and Indonesia) tigers which lie in wait for the pigs at traditional river crossings; but nothing can halt their onward progress across swift-flowing rivers, for pigs are powerful swimmers, up precipitous escarpments, and along trails that have become sunken paths under the trampling of thousands of hooves, until at some significant juncture in time or place, they reverse their migration and return to their coastal haunts.

The tigers' second major prey are deer—the medium-sized chital, now only numerous in a few forest tracts and sanctuaries; the large sambar, whose geographical distribution almost coincides with that of tigers; the rather smaller barasingha, now surviving in only a few isolated pockets of forests; and occasionally in India, but more frequently in Burma and Malaya, the muntjac, whose discordant and resonant dog-like bark, repeated again and again from some dense clump of bamboo, often gives distant warning of a tiger on the prowl, though it also barks at snakes, mongooses and monkeys. According to South American Indians, a jaguar can mimic the call of any beast or bird, and the most interesting utterance in the tiger's extensive vocabulary is one that is almost indistinguishable from the warning *pook* of a sambar stag—that loud ringing call, like the sound of a bell struck sharply, that carries for half a mile. Although a tiger often "pooks" when on guard near his kill, it is possible that he also does so with the deliberate intention of calling up a stag, for a number of Russian hunters have reported watching tigers actually call up wapiti stags in Manchuria by mimicking their rutting call: a deep bull-like bellowing that opens with a loud roar, rises a complete octave, and concludes with a bugling note. However, a tiger's repertoire also includes calls resembling the bird-like chirrup of a swamp deer and the curiously thin whining call of a bull gaur, which nevertheless can be heard a mile away at dawn and dusk, and throughout the night at the peak of the rut, and which Schaller has described as a clear, resonant, 10-second *u-u-u-u* that may be followed by a series of lower notes, as if the gaur was practicing musical scales.

The tigers' third major prey are antelope, especially the horse-sized, blue-gray bulls and tawny cows of the nilghai; perhaps as many of these as chital were formerly killed in dry deciduous forest and the thorn scrub of Rajputana. In India, tigers rarely hunt by day, mainly because it is too hot both for them and for the deer which lie up in heavy covert, as the boars do in their grass arbors, though some chital and nilghai begin feeding an hour or two before sunset; but in quiet jungles of Burma, Assam, Indo-China and Malaya that are shaded from the direct rays of the sun, and are also thinly inhabited by villagers and

Tiger

jungle aboriginals, tigers hunt as readily by day as by night. The Indian tiger usually begins hunting a little before sunset, his hide shining like burnished copper in the red glow of the evening sun as he steals through the yellowing grass. Wherever practicable he keeps to the dry beds of nullahs, and to fire-breaks, forest paths and jungle roads, all of which are free from the leeches, ticks and flies that infest heavy jungle; and in the morning his tracks can be followed for miles along these jungle highways, which were first trampled by elephants and sub-sequently made permanent by buffalo and deer. His great head, jaws parted, sways a little from side to side, and is carried low, accentuating the prodigious humps of muscle on nape and shoulders, as he paces along noiselessly with undulating 3-foot strides on cushioned pads and toes, with the sinews rippling on power-ful forearms. His long tail, upturned at its tip, swishes idly to and fro, as he glides and flows along with near fore and hind legs moving almost as one. At frequent intervals he stops to listen intently, head on one side, quickly slipping into cover if he locates a deer or sounder of pigs; while from time to time he makes a detour to investigate a water-hole, where he may lie up to await game coming to drink.

Although there are instances of tigers ham-stringing the for-midable buffalo, gaur and seladang, it is their calves on which they prey mainly, for only a very hungry tiger would be bold enough to engage a herd of these great cattle formed up in their defensive "square." However, there have been instances of a tiger and tigress combining to attack an adult elephant, and ele-phant calves are probably killed more often than is generally recognized. Under normal conditions, when an elephant is about to give birth other females in the herd usually take up positions in a circle at some distance from the lying-in place, keeping contact by calls, and presenting a more or less impregnable defensive ring against any marauding tiger. Elephants are, in any case, sensitive to small vibrations transferred through the ground to their feet, and can detect a tiger moving upwind at a considerable distance.

Associating in herds that are probably composed of large family groups that have been in existence for generations, elephant society is matriarchal. In his biography of that exceptional hunter-naturalist, Jim Hislop, sometime chief game warden in Malaya, the Australian author, Ronald McKie, describes how while the herd feeds, Granny is on guard:

> Every few minutes she stops chewing to sample the wind with her waving trunk or fans her ears forward to listen. If she scents or hears danger, or if she is suspicious, she thumps her air-distended trunk on the ground and makes a hollow metallic tapping. At this signal the herd stops moving, stops chewing, is silent—even the babies—and every trunk, every ear is alert for sound or scent. If granny is satisfied she moves on or chews and the herd relaxes. But if she senses real danger she hurries away and the herd follows her, so silently and so swiftly that the soundlessness is uncanny . . . in the herd's passing not a leaf will be shaken or rustled, not a twig broken.

In Indonesia elephants could be said to have an ecological relationship with tigers, in as much as the wastage from the leafy branches they break off attracts deer; but when the elephants move out of the deer's grazing territories the latter turn back along the elephants' trails in which they are ambushed by tigers. In Malaya wild pig take advantage of ground and bush cleared by elephants, and in some parts of India the latter frequently associate with gaur and benefit them by pulling down within their reach high foliage and bamboo shoots. In other districts, however, the gaur evacuate their feeding grounds when a herd of elephants moves in, and there have been instances of these great cattle actually attacking elephants.

Asiatic elephants, which are smaller both in stature and tusk than the savanna elephants of Africa, with bulls seldom taller than 10 feet or weighing more than 6 tons, have remained almost exclusively forest animals, though in Vietnam they migrate from the forests on the high plateaus to the plains as soon as the rainy season begins and the vegetation on the latter has recovered from the annual bush-fires; and the 250 square miles of the Lagna savannas, north-east of Saigon, formerly attracted elephants from many parts of Indo-China. In Malaya the few hundred that survive range over ancestral territories as much as 200 square miles in extent, following an approximate routine of feeding in the afternoon, bathing in the evening, feeding again until after midnight, when they sleep for three hours or so in brief spells during the night, before feeding again until their midday rest period. Elephants also catnap when standing idly, or even when chewing, and McKie observes that:

A resting herd is always silent except for two things: elephants snore, and they never stop flapping their ears, even in sleep. The convulsive flapping . . . can be heard for thirty or forty yards . . . even above the clamour of the cicadas and other noisy insects. An elephant lying asleep on its side flaps its free ear. But the sound this makes is more than a flap; it's a distinct hard slap as the ear, which weighs pounds, falls back against the grey, wrinkled, hairy hide. Even when a herd is asleep or catnapping they receive warning signals. They suddenly stop flapping . . . and stand or lie without movement. Then the sentinel . . . signals again and they all flap together as if in relief.

But although they may stay in one locality for several days while feeding on bamboo shoots or the long green beans of the kerayong trees, their immense daily requirements prevent them from remaining too long in one place, and sooner or later they must move on, covering 20 miles in a night if disturbed. Their new destination may be a grove of fruit trees or the locality of a certain creeping plant which is reputedly a heart stimulant, and after feeding on which a herd travels long distances: whereas after feeding on the possibly soporific, nutty pith of bayas palms, which they push over and stamp into pulp, they are said to become lethargic and often sleep.

At this point one must ask, how can such a large animal as the tapir survive in the jungles of Burma and Malaya virtually unmolested by predators? Although like its South American relatives, capable of inflicting a severe bite, it apparently makes no attempt to defend itself when attacked and must be regarded as more defenseless than a chital doe. Yet there are extraordinarily few records of tapirs being killed by tigers. It is true that a tapir's curious color pattern of black head, neck, withers and legs, contrasting sharply with the pure white of the remainder of its body, is disruptive and renders it inconspicuous in its heavy jungle habitat where checkered light and shade fall irregularly, while when lumbering past with head held low in a swift gallop, it appears grayish; but since tapirs feed on leaves, shoots and fruit at night, and tigers also hunt mainly at night, this camouflage would be operative only in moonlight when the white midsection does not appear to belong to an animal, since the black portions remain obscure. The tapir's acute senses of smell and hearing and its extreme wariness are probably more protective than its disruptive color pattern. Salt-licks—so essential to the health of both herbivores and carnivores—are, for example, visited by it only if no other animals are present and, of course, at night. But perhaps its most effective defense against predators is its ability to remain submerged for long periods on the bottom of a river. A paragraph from an old copy of the *Rangoon Gazette*, quoted by Dillon Ripley, sums up this little-known animal:

> The tapir is a perpetual refutation of the general application of theories on the struggle for existence. It is a shy and mild and gentle creature. . . . It is nothing much to look at and its white overcoat is an amusing vagary of jungle fashion. . . . It is not poached, the jungle people regarding it, as is the fate of many philosophers living out of their time, with almost amused contempt. . . . The tapir is in fact an enigma. It may be a survivor of some more gentle and legendary time, or it may be wandering in unique isolation in a world not yet mature enough for its wisdom.

Tigers, like jaguars and leopards, are often obliged to be omnivorous and when game is scarce a tiger will eat almost anything—grasshoppers and locusts, beetles, scorpions, frogs, crabs, fish, turtles and tortoises, crocodiles, pythons, lizards (including the large varanus monitors which gorge upon almost every tiger kill in parts of Indonesia and Indo-China), even pangolins despite their ability to roll up "impregnably," and especially porcupines, whose meat tigers are reputed to prefer to that of any other animal except pig. Porcupines are extremely numerous at night in forests and plantations, shambling along in pairs and families at an unexpectedly rapid 300 yards a minute, while puffing, moaning, mewing, booming or neighing, and quite often shuffling around tigers' kills with an aggressive rattling of the hollow quills at the ends of their tails. These tail quills have thin stems supporting open-ended cuplets or tubes, and can be likened to miniature wine-glasses with extremely elongated bowls. There is good evidence that water is carried in these quills, but whether deliberately, as has been suggested, for the purpose of cooling and laying the dust in their burrows, which may be more than 60 feet long, is another matter.

Seven species of porcupines, from the small brush-tails killed by so many leopards to the large crested 60-pounders, range through Africa and Asia to the tigers' nothern limits in Ussuriland. None are easy prey, and many a tiger has paid with its life for its folly in attacking these pugnacious and agile little beasts. In their total fearlessness of the largest carnivores, porcupines remind one of ratels, and there is one record of a porcupine actually attacking a leopard drinking at the same pool, and forcing it to retreat. According to Peter Turnbull-Kemp a porcupine's quills are soft at birth but harden into defensive weapons within ten days or so. Thereafter, a proportion of the total complement of 20,000 or 30,000 quills are continually being shed and replaced. They vary considerably in length and shape, those that are thick and of medium length being the ones that are fatal to carnivores, whereas those that are long and thin are not rigid enough to penetrate an aggressor's skin. The porcupine's defensive technique is to rush backwards, or sideways, with spines erected and make sudden severe jabs at its assailant; and the Indian naturalist, Balakrishna Seshadri, comments that, "The erection of their quills, the tremendous extrusion of air from their nostrils, the rattling of their hollow tail quills, and the final launching backwards of the whole body is a very potent destructive process. This backward movement is a lightning-like affair . . . in which the quills are thrust into the body of the would-be attacker and released by muscular movement."

In attacking such small prey, a tiger is liable to make the fatal error of attempting to bite them or strike them with its paw, and there are many records of tigers found dead with the needle-pointed quills of porcupines embedded in paws, mouth, throat, neck or chest, and even under the skin of the back, or with livers and lungs perforated like sieves. More often the quills cause permanent and crippling disability, for as their barbs become moistened they expand slightly and, once embedded, muscular contractions result in deeper penetration; moreover they never dissolve. A tiger wounded in this way is unable to stalk and kill its normal prey, and is likely to become a man-eater. Leopards, on the other hand, which kill many more porcupines than tigers do, catch them by their heads, on which the spines are not as stiff. Nevertheless, many are injured, and there is at least one record of one of these turning man-eater.

Leopards, despite their extraordinary strength and incomparable agility, are sometimes killed by tigers, though they often poach from the latter's kills; and in jungles where tigers are numerous leopards "cache" their own kills in trees, as they also do on lion-infested savannas. However, leopards and tigers do not compete for prey in jungles that are adequately stocked with game, because tigers concentrate on the larger types of prey, and leopards on the smaller. Only "specialist" leopards attempt to kill prey as large as wild pigs, by which they are indeed sometimes tree'd. But if game is scarce, then leopards must give way to tigers and move out to other jungles.

In all their habitats tigers play a vital role as controllers of animal populations, and just as the large-scale slaughter of leopards in Africa has resulted in an immense increase in the numbers of destructive baboons, so the even more widespread extermination of tigers in Asia has had similar effects. Not only do both tigers and leopards kill more crop-destroying game than domestic cattle, but their mere presence near villages deters deer, pig and monkeys from encroaching upon fields and plantations. In both India and Malaya the wholesale felling of forests has not only deprived the remaining predators of their covert, but has also led to the concentration of deer and pig in or near cultivated areas, and the invasion of these areas by hordes of monkeys.

15: In the Gum Forests of Australia

In the context of this book the two outstanding facts about Australia are that only one-fifth of the continent is forested, and that this forest area, of which only 1 per cent is rain-forest, is dominated by some 50 species of eucalyptus or gum trees, ranging from low bushes to giants such as the blue gums and the white-barked mountain ashes and karris whose straight boles tower to heights of 300 or 375 feet. Few are less than 500 feet tall and, since their crowns do not form a compact canopy, sufficient sunlight penetrates to nourish a rich undergrowth; older trees are gnarled and battered, and scarred where branches have broken off, with rounded knobs in the hollows of which birds nest and possums roost. The gums have been able to colonize almost every kind of country, except the rain-forest from which they are normally absent, but dominate two main types of temperate forest. One is wet and low-lying with a marked or luxuriant undergrowth of shrubs or, in more humid regions at lower altitudes, of tree-ferns and palms; while the other, at higher altitudes, has a less dense shrubbery. In contrast to the broad leaves, displaying maximum surfaces for chlorophyll synthesis, of rain-forest trees, the drab-blue or gray-green leaves of gums are long and narrow with thick shiny skins, and tend to hang with their surfaces away from the sun. Loss of moisture by evaporation is thus reduced to a minimum, and the leaves remain on the trees throughout the most prolonged drought.

The eucalyptus flora is inseparably associated with Australia's dominant fauna, the great variety of marsupial or pouched animals which fill nearly all the roles of animals in other parts of the world. Their distribution is influenced by that of the gums, and many could not exist without them. They range from small plant-eaters to successful predators; and such diverse mammals as dogs, moles, and flying-squirrels all have their marsupial counterparts. The gums flower erratically, usually at intervals of two or three years, and do not bear fruit; but when they do flower, their abundant heavy-scented blossoms, mainly white but also red, orange or yellow, attract hosts of nectar-seeking birds; and more than half of the world's 160 species of honey-eaters inhabit Australia, especially the Sunshine Coast of Queensland, where gums and such honeysuckles as the banksia or wallum provide an ample reserve of food during the colder winter months.

Feeding on different species of gums at different seasons, the honey-eaters are possibly their main pollinators, as they are of the wallum, from whose large, stiff, brush-like flowers flow quantities of reputedly intoxicating nectar. Since the rich nectar of the petal-less gum blossom collects at the center of the flower in a shallow basin surrounded by large numbers of erect and curved pollen-bearing stamens, the honey-eaters come into contact with the latter, with the result that their heads often become coated with a yellowish or white accumulation of pollen. In order to extract the nectar from its recess the honey-eaters have evolved various devices. The tip of the yellow-fronted species' protrusible tongue is, for example, split into four parts with delicately frayed edges forming a brush with which to procure the nectar; this is then channeled along a groove in the base of the rather long beak.

Flying-foxes also feed on the nectar-bearing blossoms of gums and possibly prefer them to fruit, pressing the juice out of the blossoms in their mouths. Colonizing Australia from their original home in New Guinea, though still migrating seasonally to remain within warm latitudes, they have been able to build up enormous populations, congregating at day camps, some of which have been occupied for more than fifty years, in colonies of upwards of a million; but these camps are usually located in rain-forest or mangroves and only rarely in the gums, to which they forage over a radius of 10 or 20 miles from their camps, attracted by the scent of the flowers.

Gum trees also provide other sources of food, such as the seed capsules of the marri or red gum which are exploited by three members of the parrot family—the black palm cockatoo, which is no relation to the giant black cockatoo of New Guinea and the Aru Islands, and which is represented in Australia only by a small colony in north Queensland; the king or red-capped parrot, resplendent with pea-green face, green back and wings and purple underparts, which is equipped with a very long, thin lower mandible with which to hook the nuts out of their capsules; and the twenty-eight parrot which chews the capsules. These parrots, with their upper mandibles jointed and movable as an aid to climbing trees, are the woodpeckers of Australia and New Guinea, securing the larvae of wood-boring insects that infest the gum trees by tearing off the bark with their huge beaks, as do those large brownish New Zealand parrots, the kakas. However, in addition to their powerful beaks, the latter also possess, surprisingly, brush-fringed tongues with which to suck up gum from beneath the bark or nectar from such flowers as the crimson rata. The most powerful of all is the giant black cockatoo, blue-black or slate-gray with naked blood-red cheeks, and more than 2 feet long. This bird shatters the marri capsules with its monstrous hooked and sharp-pointed beak, 4 inches long, which is capable of crunching a china bowl into small pieces or, more practically, of crushing the smooth, somewhat triangular-shaped nuts of the kanari tree in order to extract the kernels. No other bird can cope with these nuts; not surprisingly, since a man can only do so with the aid of a heavy hammer. Alfred Russell Wallace has left us a characteristically exact account of the ingenious technique employed by this cockatoo in opening a kanari nut:

> Taking one endways in its bill and keeping it firm by a pressure of the somewhat prehensile tongue, it cuts a transverse notch by a lateral sawing motion of the sharp-edged lower mandible. This done, it takes hold of the nut with its foot, and biting off a piece of leaf retains it in the deep notch of the upper mandible, and again seizing the nut, which is prevented from slipping by the elastic tissue of the leaf, fixes the edge of the lower mandible in the notch, and by a powerful nip breaks off a piece of the shell. Again taking in the nut in its claws, it inserts the very long and sharp point of the bill and picks out the kernel, which is seized hold of, morsel by morsel, by the prehensile red tongue, which is tubular and terminates in a horny black plate.

The gliding possums, which are almost exclusively arboreal, and not related to the American opossums, are probably also significant pollinators of gum trees, though they are insectivorous too, while some, such as brush-tails and cuscuses, are partially carnivorous. The large sugar-gliders which, in addition to feeding on flowers and fruits, score the bark of the manna or sugar-gums with their teeth and lick the small sugary lumps of congealed sap, have successfully colonized eucalyptus forests and open woodlands over large areas of Australia. Both the pygmy feather-tail gliders and the pygmy honey-possums extract nectar from the blossoms of gums and wallum, and also catch nectar-feeding insects (and termites) with lightning leaps, and both nest in the hollow branches of gums. The honey-possum indeed relapses into a state of almost total torpidity during the cold months, when blossoms and insects are scarce, subsisting on its body and tail fat; for, like the honey-eating birds, it has become almost completely adapted to procuring nectar and pollen. Its teeth have degenerated and its elongated snout has become modified into a proboscis suitable for thrusting into the blossoms of the tea-tree and around the cones of the bottle-brush; for when its mouth is partly closed small overlapping flanges on the lower lip form a tube through which nectar and pollen can be sucked, while the long, thin, bristly tongue with a tuft at its tip can be protruded an inch or more and thrust deep into a bell-shaped flower to sweep up the nectar. Feeding while hanging upside down by its whip-like prehensile tail from the slenderest twigs—for it is only 6 inches long, including 3 inches of tail—it laps so rapidly that its tongue seems to vibrate. The Australian naturalist, Graham Pizzey, was puzzled by the fact that the honey-possum's eyes are situated so high on its head; but when he placed one on a wallum he saw that it plunged its snout so deeply into the bloom that only its eyes and sensitive ears remained exposed: "After a moment it withdrew a snout golden with honey, ran nimbly down a branch to the next flower, and sank its proboscis once more into it. This action . . . wiped off some of the pollen on to the new flower."

All the possums are equipped with climbing aids in the form of strong nails, though their great toes are actually nail-less and opposable to the other toes when they are grasping branches; but they are also able to make controlled glides for considerable

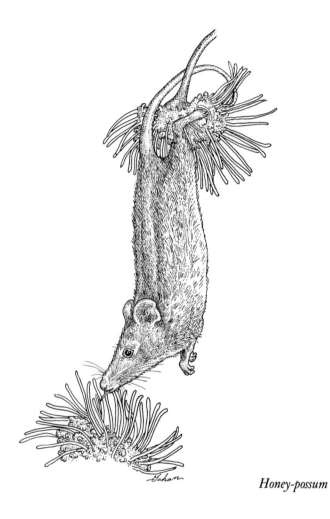

Honey-possum

distances from tree to tree, like flying-squirrels, with their hair-fringed tails acting as rudders. The honey-possum, for example, can capture moths while gliding, and the sugar-glider can change direction in the course of its 40 or 50 yards "flight" to alight on a different tree to the one at which it was originally aimed. The greater glider, which is 3 feet in length inclusive of its long fluffy tail, can cover a distance of as much as 120 yards from the top of one tree to the base of another, though its landing curve is so low that it is liable to impale itself on barbed-wire fencing. The gliding possums also make use of their tails to collect nesting material. Suspended upside down by its hind-feet in the moonlight, a sugar-glider bites the leaves off gum twigs, transfers them with its forepaws to its tail, which coils around them, and then runs along the branches with its bundle of material to its nest.

Even more dependent than possums on gum trees for its very existence is the banded ant-eater or numbat, a striped, rat-sized marsupial, not unlike a squirrel when in excitement it curves its bushy tail over its back. Not only do the gums supply the solitary-living numbats with their sole source of food, but also with essential shelter and refuges. They are especially associated with the white gum or wandoo, which is the dominant tree in their restricted habitat, the shrubby woodlands of south-west Australia. During weather changes large numbers of heavy branches break off the wandoos, and the forest floor is permanently strewn with their hollow limbs and boughs. Since the annual rainfall in this region amounts to only 20 inches these hollow limbs remain intact for many years, and provide the numbats with homes and sleeping places on beds of dead leaves and grasses. Moreover, the wandoos also support large populations of termites, especially the *Coptotermes acinaciformis* which are the most abundant and destructive species in south-west Australia and have eaten the heart out of almost all mature gums over large areas of woodland. Since a daily intake of possibly 10,000 or 20,000 termites forms 85 per cent of a numbat's food, it follows that it can only live where large numbers of these are available, for the remaining 15 per cent is composed of small predatory ants that swarm into the termites' galleries when these are exposed, and are probably mainly ingested fortuitously by the numbat when it is feeding on the termites.

Because a numbat is not strong enough to break open termitaries, it procures its termites from their gallery runways in the upper couple of inches of soil or in cracks in fallen boughs. Its most profitable feeding places are within a few feet of a termitary or of the base of a large wandoo, where the soil is damp and friable and contains quantities of leaf-litter and bark, and also alongside partly embedded logs or partly exposed tree roots, though it is a good climber and often probes for termites high up in dead trees. Locating a gallery by its strong eucalyptus odor, the numbat digs down very rapidly with its long claws, opening a vertical shaft an inch or two deep, or scratches into a rotten log, levering pieces apart with its long thin snout, and intrudes 4 inches of cylindrical sticky tongue. One wonders on what prey numbats originally fed with their extraordinary complement of fifty or fifty-two now degenerate teeth.

There has been a drastic decline in the numbers of numbats, and this has been generally attributed to bush fires and the introduced red foxes. But J. H. Calaby, who made a two years' study of numbats, concluded that the role of predators in this decline had been greatly exaggerated. He found no evidence that numbats were preyed on to any significant extent by either hawks or foxes; foxes are in any case mainly nocturnal hunters, whereas numbats are normally diurnal, except on hot summer days. If they are subject to predation, then this is more likely to be by goanna lizards and carpet-pythons, for these would be able to follow numbats into the narrow cracks in logs which their attenuated, almost reptilian form enables them to use as escape-holes. Calaby also concluded that bush fires were not the cause of the numbats' decline, because these are of rare occurrence in their woodland habitat, while controlled forestry burning does not affect trees or sound hollow logs, and leaves the majority of termitaries unaffected. In his opinion, land clearance for agricultural purposes and the removal of hollow logs, the numbats' only refuge, are the main threat to their survival.

If numbats could not exist in a habitat lacking the hollow logs and termitaries associated with the white gums, there could similarly be no koalas without gum trees, for the latter's food requirements are more specialized than those of any other mammal. With the exception of small amounts of mineral soil a koala's diet is believed to be restricted to the leaves of a bare dozen of the 350 species of gums growing within its habitat, and especially to five with smooth bark and a high oil content, including the manna, candle-bark, yellow box and swamp gums; while in order to process this tough vegetable matter, of which it consumes 2½ pounds daily, it has developed an appendix 6 or 8 feet long and two or three times as long as its body. Liquids are apparently obtained from the gum leaves—the koala is said to derive its name from the aboriginal *kuala*, "no drink"—and fresh or salt water upsets captive koalas, though they can take milk-and-water. Moreover, koalas of different regions do not eat the leaves of the same species of gums, whose taste and nutriment are influenced by local soils. The leaves of most gums contain cineol, which is known to decrease blood pressure and body temperature and relax the muscles, and also phellandren, which is believed to increase body temperature; and koalas in the warm forests of northern Queensland are reputed to avoid trees with excessive phellandren and feed on those with a higher content of cineol, while the larger race of koalas inhabiting the cooler forests of southern Australia reverse this preference. Furthermore, koalas are such skilled analysts that they can discriminate between the leaves on a single tree, for the leaves of some gums are toxic at certain stages of growth and at certain seasons. The manna, for example, produces a higher content of hydrocyanic (prussic) acid in winter than in summer, and also in its young leaves and shoots, and this acid is released by chemical action when the leaves are masticated. Rather than eat the manna's leaves when they are toxic the koalas change their food trees, traveling considerable distances on the ground at night in search of fresh trees.

Normally, a koala rarely begins feeding until 10 o'clock in the morning, and when it has eaten all the suitable leaves on a tree it usually climbs out along a branch until this sways into the foliage of an adjoining tree and it can make a frantic leap into its new feeding quarters; but if this is not practicable it makes a slow backward descent to the ground, and then runs rapidly to the next tree. With one toe larger than the others, the index fingers of its hands opposable, and nails as sharp as knives, it can bound swiftly up a broad trunk.

When a female koala is three years old she begins to produce single young ones, usually in alternate years. Though less than 1 inch long and only $1/5$ of an ounce in weight at birth and, like the young of other marsupials, still a partially developed blind and naked embryo, the newly-born koala is nevertheless immediately able to crawl through its mother's fur to her pouch and attach itself to the nipple; but, still more extraordinary, when it is five weeks old, it begins to feed on a predigested liquid mess of leaves which it obtains from its mother's anus. This it continues to do every second or third day over a period of five weeks, and it is able to do this because the opening of the pouch faces the anus, as it does in the female wombat; though in her case as a preventative against soil being flung into the pouch when she is digging. When six or seven months old the young koala migrates from the pouch to its mother's back, where it remains for another six months before leaving her altogether. It will be full-grown when four years old, with the chance of surviving in its small area of gum trees for a further eight or perhaps sixteen years.

Pizzey has hazarded the suggestion that, although they are now so different, koalas were perhaps originally wombats that graduated to an arboreal way of life. Some 3 feet long and 100 pounds in weight, a wombat has the chisel-like front teeth of a beaver, which it somewhat resembles except for its lack of a tail, and can gnaw through the toughest roots. Rapid diggers with their powerful shovel-shaped claws, the wombats' deep fireproof burrows up to 100 feet long, together with their ability to subsist on roots and bark, and also grass and fungi, have enabled them to survive the bush fires that ravage Australia year in and year out.

Consolidating the sand-dunes from central New South Wales to south-west Australia is a different kind of forest—a rolling gray-green ocean of trees, composed of several dozen species of dwarf and stunted gums, collectively known as the Mallee. This is a region with an annual rainfall of less than 12 inches, but the gums siphon water from the arid soil through taproots and also, by means of additional sub-surface roots, collect the moisture that drips on to the sand from dew condensing on their waxy down-pointing leaves. Moreover, in order that its sparse foliage shall provide maximum shade for its roots, the mallee gum does not have the single trunk of the typical eucalyptus but sprouts in multiple slender stems to a height of 10 or 12 feet above the surrounding shrubbery and porcupine grass, from an underground ligno-tuber, which serves as an additional store of water and plant food, and can survive both drought and fire.

This harsh country is the habitat of one of the world's more remarkable birds—the mallee-fowl—which, like the brush-tur-keys and scrub-fowl of tropical forest, is a megapode. Because the pullet-sized female mallee-fowl, weighing only 3½ pounds, lays a 7- or 8-ounce egg at intervals of from 2 to 17 days over a per-iod of from 4 to 6 months, she obviously cannot also incubate her eggs. On the other hand, since temperatures in the Mallee country may fall by more than 60 degrees F between noon and midnight, and since there is insufficient moisture to guarantee fermentation in the "compost heap" that other megapodes em-ploy as incubators, it devolves on the male mallee-fowl to operate an incubator for his mate's extended clutch of as many as forty eggs. To this end, both birds co-operate, at the time of the first late-autumn or early-winter rains, in excavating a crater-like depression, 2 or 3 feet deep, in sandy soil. This they fill with leaves, twigs and grasses, cleaning up the surrounding area and raking material backwards from distances of 50 yards or more, until the mound of vegetation rises a couple of feet above ground level and is as much as 18 feet in diameter, con-taining barrow-loads of material. By comparison the average brush-turkey's mound is 12 feet in diameter and 3 or 4 feet high, though these dimensions have apparently been greatly exceeded by scrub-fowl, one of which is reported to have scratched some 9,000 cubic feet of soil and debris into a mound 15 feet high and about 150 feet in diameter under a giant fig tree in the Arnhem Land jungle.

Once the brush-turkeys and scrub-fowl have constructed their mounds and laid their eggs in them, their work is finished, for the eggs will incubate and the young hatch without further at-tention; whereas the male mallee-fowl, who sometimes works alone, rehabilitating a previous year's mound, is only at the beginning of his prolonged and extraordinary labors. By mid-winter the rains have dampened and rotted down the vegetative material in his mound. As spring advances it begins to heat up, and the male in particular visits the mound every morning and scratches more and more sand over it, eventually burying it beneath a layer of soil 2 or 3 feet deep. By doing this he ensures that fermentative action liberates sufficient heat to produce a temperature of about 92 degrees F a few inches below the surface. The mallee-fowl are able to achieve this critical temperature, which is within a degree or two of the incubatory temperature of various species of conventionally nesting birds, in both the coolest and hottest parts of their range, and in certain localities take advantage of the soil being heated by thermal springs or volcanic activity.

Early in the spring the male is warned by his mate's agitation that she is ready to lay her first egg; but if she attempts to lay in unsuitable conditions, when the sun is too hot or when cold rain is falling, and opening up the mound would have an adverse effect on the internal temperature, he chases her away and she is obliged to drop her egg elsewhere. But if conditions are suitable he opens up the mound by first scratching back its covering of sand and then scooping out a hole in the under layer of vegetation, while repeatedly testing the internal temperature by ramming his head down and plunging his beak, with its sensitive bare skin, into the "compost" for a second or two. When he has worked his way down to the fermenting pad of leaf mold, the female takes his place and, after some preparatory settling down, straddles the shallow hole and lays her egg directly into it. According to Pizzey, she then scrapes a few clawfuls of sand around the egg and wanders off into the bush, usually leaving the male to re-seal the mound and to continue working on it day and night, regulating its temperature. He sleeps near it and feeds near it, obtaining essential liquids for his own use from insects and small moisture-containing herbs, and tests the mound's temperature with his beak several times every day. In cool, windy or wet weather he heaps up sand over the mound to blanket developing heat. In warm weather, when there is too much combustion at midday, he opens up holes in the mound or scratches the sand-covering down from the sides in the very early morning so that it may be chilled, and then, when it has cooled, piles it over the mound again. As the season advances, however, the compost burns itself out and fermentation gradually ceases. The summer sun is now the main source of heat, and the mallee-fowl, with an inexplicable instinctive knowledge of chemical processes, again spreads out the mound's sand-covering in the morning and also later in the day until the sun has heated it, when it is piled back on the mound again.

Despite summer heat in excess of 100 degrees F, this astonishing, by no means large, bird labors constantly at shifting several hundredweights of sand. Although we do not know how he is able to gauge the mound temperature correctly—he appears to sample beakfuls of material—we do know that the temperature of the compost in artificial mounds constructed experimentally initially soars as high as 106 degrees F and then, having exhausted its combustibility, sinks well below the critical level. Only the daily attentions of the mallee-fowl can maintain the required temperature constantly over a period long enough to hatch his mate's full clutch of eggs. His continual presence at the mound may, incidentally, prevent goanna lizards from raiding the eggs and also from laying their own eggs in it.

There are usually six or eight eggs in the mound at one time in different stages of development, but although, during the course of her intermittent laying, the female mallee-fowl seldom uncovers eggs laid previously, she nevertheless succeeds in depositing them in a pattern variously described as roughly symmetrical or remarkably even, thus ensuring an unobstructed exit route for each chick when, after six or eight weeks' incubation, it fractures the wafer-thin shell and embarks on a struggle to the surface of the mound that may last from three to seventeen hours. Some chicks are suffocated before they can break out, but those that emerge successfully are well developed and fully feathered and able, after resting, to totter down off the mound into the shelter of the scrub. Within an hour they can run, feed on insects and small plants, and clamber and flutter up to branches to roost, and within twenty-four hours can fly. When the last of the young mallee-fowl break out of the incubator the male's herculean labors cease after some eleven months; but the first autumn showers preceding the winter rains bring him back to the nesting territory once again to clear out the "dead" compost and begin preparations for another season's prolonged activity. For how many seasons, one wonders, can a mallee-fowl sustain such unremitting toil?

Another remarkable bird inhabits the more densely forested, rugged country of south-eastern Australia, where giant gums climb from steep gullies to mountain tops, and fast-flowing, ice-cold streams are almost concealed by cascading masses of magnificent green tree-ferns and fringed with blackwoods, wattles, myrtles and heavily perfumed musks and sassafras. Here lives the superb lyre-bird—a bantam-sized bird, ash-brown in color relieved by red on the wings and adorned, in the case of the male, by a 2-foot-long tail formed of twelve lacy feathers encompassing two gracefully curved, lyre-shaped plumes. With their strong legs and enormous feet and claws, the lyre-birds demolish large sections of decaying logs, and rake deep in the soil for earthworms, centipedes, snails, the large white grubs of beetles and ghost-moths, and small crustaceans which infest the humus at densities of from 8 to 40 per square foot. When the ridges and upper slopes of the gum forests dry out and the ground hardens in hot summ*r*s, the lyre-birds migrate down into the dank ferny gullies. In the autumn, however, the male begins that season of song and display for which he is famed. Staking out a territory, from 3 to 10 acres in extent and a quarter of a mile from that of his nearest neighbor, he scratches up as many as a dozen low earth-mounds, 3 feet in diameter, within the shade of ferns and shrubbery. On these mounds, or sometimes on logs, he spends a part of every winter's day in song and display, hopping backward and forward in stiff, measured hops. His performance reaches a peak, strangely enough, with the lessening hours of daylight, falling temperatures and increasing rainfall of early winter, and he sings most ardently in misty weather with a drizzle of rain. His song attracts any female in the vicinity, though once they have mated she wanders off alone into the bush to build her large domed nest and rear her chicks without any assistance from the male. Pizzey has described the males as "fabulous mimics, weaving the calls of several dozen other birds, together with their own repeated phrases into a ringing torrent of song"; and we can conclude this chapter with his account of an incident when a male he was watching burst into song in a clearing containing four display mounds, another male rushed up the hill:

> The bird was facing us, pouring out his song, while his breath clouded in the freezing air. I crouched six feet away from him. . . . At this range each note hit my ear like a small hammer blow. . . . Then the bird began to imitate. He started with the "cracking" sound of the coach-whip bird, followed by the small silver notes of the pilot birds, and then the laughter of the kookaburra. We heard the wild scream of the black cockatoo, and the squabbling of a flock of rosella parrots, and even the rustle of their wings. . . . The bird's voice suddenly altered. I looked up and saw a female lyre-bird approaching through the bracken . . . the male swung his great tail for-

ward over his head [in her direction]. One moment it had
been folded, a profusion of gleaming black and russet, and the
next it was a shimmering silver umbrella completely envelop-
ing the bird, the two lyrate plumes forming a single curve
. . . swaying slightly, he pours out his rising song. . . . The
umbrella was violently shaken, and the dance began. A per-
cussion-like *blick-blick-blick-blick* rang through the forest, interspersed with an extraordinary *chungada, chungada* which
sounded as if it were being beaten out on small, leathery
drums. At each beat the bird dipped, clapping his wings
against his sides in rhythm.

16: Bower-Birds and Birds of Paradise

The display of the superb lyre-bird leads us to the still more remarkable activities of the bower-birds and birds of paradise, and to the montane rain-forests of New Guinea in particular with their arboreal gardens of orchids and endless mazes of vines and creepers. Fantastic crowned pigeons, the size of capercaillies, with fan-shaped slate-blue crests, scarlet eyes, light slate-blue and rufous plumage, white wings with a rufous stripe, and red feet, feed on fallen fruits and berries. Numerous forms of cassowaries, each in its ½-mile or 2-mile territory, stalk warily through the densest forest, also in search of fruit and berries. Protected by nictating eyelids, horny helmets and a tough cloak-like plumage of uncovered quills, with no webbing to catch in and be torn by thornbush, they can run through the most compacted undergrowth without becoming entangled or suffering injury.

In the mountain forests are tree kangaroos with capes of dark-brown fur, growing outwards from a whorl near the shoulders, to protect them from the torrential rains when they are hunched up asleep with their heads bowed. Their very large hands, sharp curved claws and roughened hairy pads enable these small kangaroos to be truly arboreal and at home in the highest branches, climbing very large trees by means of the festoons of vines; leaping 30 feet from branch to branch, when the long possum-like tail with a thick brush at its tip acts as a rudder (and also as a prop when climbing); and plummeting 50 or 60 feet to the ground if alarmed, when the soles of their large hind-feet, cushioned by a thick layer of fat under the skin, act as shock absorbers. Although they pass much of their time on the forest floor, feeding on ferns, vines and fruit, they are slow movers, progressing in relatively short hops with forefeet touching the ground, for their hind limbs are much less powerfully developed than those of typical kangaroos, and little longer than their forelimbs.

As in Australia, monkeys are replaced by possums; and flying-foxes, huge honking hornbills and screaming cockatoos are the inhabitants of the treetops, while tiny green, stiff-tailed parrots, no larger than wrens and peculiar to New Guinea, take the place of woodpeckers, hopping up the trunks with both feet together and using their stiff tail-feathers as a support. Reference has previously been made to the way some animals have put termitaries to use, and Sten Bergman, a Swedish explorer, has recorded finding three nests of these dwarf parrots actually built within occupied termitaries. One was an oval, unlined nest-chamber, 8 inches long and 6 inches high, constructed slightly below center in the heart of an unusually round termitary 11 feet up a large fig tree, and the parrots gained access to their nest through a hole in the bottom of the termitary. In a second instance a funnel-shaped entry-hole had been hacked out low on the side of a 5-foot-long termitary built 3 feet above the ground on a tree stump. All three nests were occupied for no less than thirteen or fourteen hours every night by groups of families—a most unusual arrangement—with one nest housing six adults and two nestlings, a second six adults and sub-adults, and the third five adults and sub-adults; moreover adult cocks, distinguished by an orange patch on the underparts, disgorged food not only to the nestlings, but also to sub-adults. Bergman was unable to discover what this food was, for although captive parrots ate a few termites, they did not relish them and would not eat any of the other kinds of food he provided.

Two other species of parrots also nest in termitaries, as do some kingfishers, while kookaburras, which usually nest in holes in trees, sometimes tunnel into termitaries on stumps or trunks. Bergman found a nest, 6 inches high and 9 inches wide, containing two nestlings of one kingfisher, the thrush-sized rufous, blue-green and white *Sauromarptis gaudichaud*. This had been chiseled out of an occupied termitary 10 feet up a smallish tree, and beneath it were the remains of little crabs' claws and dragonflies' wings together with the scutellum of a beetle. Michael Sharland has described how in excavating a termitary a small kingfisher:

> Takes aim from a branch, and comes smack up against the chosen spot, its momentum being the force behind the dagger point of its bill. Time and again, it makes impact at high speed . . . until it has penetrated sufficiently to get a claw hold; it then continues the excavating with short effective jabs. Once through the outer wall . . . it burrows for as much as a foot or more before forming a nest cavity inside.

Kingfishers are evidently eccentric in their choice of nesting sites, for a Malayan species has been seen carrying fish to nestlings in a large hole, situated high up in a dead tree, although a constant stream of bees were leaving and entering the hole.

In this environment live the bower-birds and birds of paradise. Of the 18 species of the former, 10 are exclusive to New Guinea and 6 to the lowland rain-forests of Australia, while 2 species occur in both regions. Although some of the New

Guinea species live at altitudes of 8,000 or 9,000 feet, the majority, like most of the birds of paradise, inhabit the mid-mountain
oak forests between 4,500 and 7,500 feet, immediately above the
rain-forest. Although some, like lyre-birds, are exceptional mimics, most are relatively drably plumaged in comparison with the
birds of paradise, and their fame lies in their unique courtship
bowers, which serve the males as pavilions in which to perform
dancing displays that will draw as many females as possible,
while the latter are perhaps additionally attracted by the archi-
tecture and colorful "furnishings" of the bowers. That this is the
probable purpose of the bowers is suggested by the fact that the
males of species with colorful plumage or ornate head plumes
tend to construct less elaborate bowers, while those species in
which both sexes are colorfully plumaged do not build bowers
but conduct their courtship in the trees, and are monogamous,
in contrast to the females of bower-building species which nest
and rear their chicks without any assistance from their polygynous mates. Since the males of some or all those species that
construct bowers mature sexually several months earlier than
the females, their urge to do so could be interpreted as the end-
result of a frustrated nest-building drive.

There are four main types of bowers. Two are relatively
primitive, merely small cleared ground spaces or courts in the
more open parts of the forest, and these courts are kept meticu-
lously clean and continually refurbished with mats of ornamen-
tal leaves and a few twigs, and/or ringed and decorated with a
variety of colorful objects. A third type, erected in a court 3 or 4
feet long and 20 or 30 inches broad, is much more elaborate,
taking the form of an avenue, 4 or 5 inches wide, with walls of
upright grass stems or sticks, 12 inches long, inserted in a rigid
mat or platform of intermeshed twigs and inclined inwards to
arch almost over the passageway. Among avenue-builders, Lau-

terbach's bower-bird, an olive-brown, thrush-sized bird with yellowish underparts, is unique in constructing avenues with four walls instead of two, and its bower may contain as many as 3,000 twigs, with 1,000 hair-like strands of grass lining the vertical walls facing the inner court. The majority of this species' bowers are decorated with red berries and a lesser number of large greenish-blue ones, while upwards of 1,000 blue-gray pebbles may be inserted between the upright twigs. An American ornithologist and photographer, E. Thomas Gilliard, has described how females, similarly plumaged to the males, entered a Lauterbach's bower three times during the many days that he watched from a hide. At their entry the male became highly excited and began to dance, and on one occasion, when a female jumped quickly within the walls and stood still and alert, he picked up a marble-sized red berry with his beak, held it high, and displayed it to her.

The best known of the bower-birds, the satin bower-bird, constructs the more usual two-walled avenue and, like some other species, usually aligns the walls north and south across the path of the sun. It has been suggested that this north-south orientation ensures that the male does not have to stare into the sun while keeping the motionless female under observation when he begins to display with widespread wings very early in the morning, while she, likewise, can watch his display without discomfort. Although this does not seem a very probable theory the correct orientation is evidently important, for if the alignment of the walls is altered experimentally, the male demolishes them and re-orientates them correctly. Having constructed his avenue, the male satin bower-bird dumps a miscellany of objects at one entrance. These may include such odd and colorful forest "jewelry" as flowers, leaves, berries, parrot feathers, iridescent insect skeletons, snake-skins, snail shells, chips of amber-colored resin or pebbles, together with such pilfered man-made objects as glass beer-bottle tops, aluminium foil, teaspoons, pieces of paper or cloth, or shot-gun shells, of which one bower-bird collected no fewer than twenty-four. Each species of bower-bird usually collects objects of predictable colors. Those of the satin bower-bird are, for example, predominantly blue or yellow, though blue, which is approximately the color of its own plumage, is preferred to yellow-green. Actually the male's plumage is basically black, but it has a strong violet-purple gloss and appears lilac-blue in sunlight, while the irises of its eyes are blue— though suffused with blood during display—and the beak is dull blue with a greenish-yellow tip.

Although one hesitates to approve the suggestion that the male selects blue objects because this is also the color of rival males, in preference to yellow-green which is the color of the females and sub-adult males, it is true that captive satin bower-birds have been known to kill small blue birds in the same aviary; while Pizzey describes how the fetish objects in the bower are "constantly arranged and rearranged, and used in bizarre threat displays in which the male hurls himself at [these] substitute rivals, pecking them furiously, displaying at them and running about them in strange, stiff-legged, eye-popping ecstasies." He suggests that these antics not only serve to attract and stimulate the females, but also give the owner of a bower a psychological edge over rival males intruding on his territory.

John Warham has described in *Animals* a no doubt typically frustrating day in the life of a bower-bird—in this instance an avenue builder with a preference for red "jewelry," the greater bower-bird:

The bird arrives at the bower in the first cool hours of the morning, announcing his approach with various hissing and mewing noises and dropping down through the bushes to the bower. Alert and beady-eyed, he begins by submitting the structure to a detailed inspection, working along the walls of the avenue and testing each stick with downward stroking movements of his open bill, straightening out any that are askew. Then he begins to shift the bones and shells about, to no obvious pattern, cocking his head to one side as if enjoying the clink as they fall back on to the pile.

Presently a female appears, smaller and drabber than the male. He now becomes quite transformed. His body becomes strangely rigid and he acquires an almost robot-like appearance as, snatching up a bone, he hops stiff-legged to the side of the bower and begins to jerk his head rhythmically up and down. He punctuates each movement with a succession of harsh ticking cries which create the impression not of a living bird but of an animated clockwork toy.

Meanwhile the female remains quietly watchful as she perches outside the end of the bower farthest from where the male is displaying. She seems both attracted and repelled by his bizarre behaviour. She flicks her wings nervously as, with a violent gesture, he flings the bone aside, grabs a fragment of glass, and continues his performance, now and then leaping high into the air. Suddenly the feathers on the nape of his neck part to reveal a crest of feathers of a silky rose-lilac hue that seems all the brighter in contrast to the dull browns and greys of the rest of his plumage. At this point he holds his head in such a way that this brightly coloured patch is visible to the female through the length of the bower, framed by one end of it.

None of this, however, lures the female into the bower—on the contrary, she now appears even more nervous. So, abandoning his head-jerking display but still moving tensely in clockwork fashion, the male hops out towards her in a wide encircling movement. Holding now a leaf in his bill he tries, with a series of powerful leaps accompanied by hisses and splutters, to drive the female into his bower. She, however, is very wary and dodges around so as to keep the bower always between them. Finally, startled by some wild movement of the male, she flies off. He at once relaxes; his bright crest is folded away again and, after a few half-hearted probings among his ornaments, he, too, departs.

Besides collecting brightly colored objects with which to adorn their bowers, the satin bower-birds and two other species paint or plaster the walls of their bowers with grass or fruit pulp, while some, though not apparently all, males of these species have learned, like the woodpecker finches of the Galápagos, to employ tools for this purpose. Collecting fragments of fibrous bark or decayed wood or charcoal resulting from a forest fire, the male chews and manipulates these with his beak until he has manufactured a small oval pellet or wad. Then, retaining the wad almost wholly within his slightly parted mandibles, he jabs at one of the upright sticks in a bower wall and paints or, rather, wipes the mess up and down the stick with the sides of his beak. This black plaster, which soon dries to a gritty charcoal powder, is replaced daily at the peak of the displaying season.

Architecturally, the most elaborate bowers are those of the fourth type, the maypoles or wigwams that tower to a height of 9 feet in some instances. It is more than a hundred years since Odoardo Beccari described how a thrush-sized, olive-brown bower-bird, the vogelkop gardener, constructs this type of bower deep in the forest on a court about 4 feet square carpeted with tree moss and adorned with colorful flowers and fruits; and his account has been confirmed more recently by Dillon Ripley. The vogelkop begins by building a small cone of moss around the base of a sapling, the size of a walking-stick, which serves as the central pillar of the wigwam. Then the thin pliant stems, 20 inches or so in length, of an arboreal orchid with fresh leaves are bent from the top of the pillar to radiate down to the ground;

Great gray bower-birds

and finally the structure, 3 feet in height, is intermeshed transversely with more stems to form an impermeable tepee from 3 to 5 feet in diameter, while a rounded aperture, a foot high, at ground level affords entry to the circular chamber within. Ripley has described the garden-like appearance of a vogelkop's court:

> This curious structure fronted on the cleared area. The impression of a front lawn was heightened by several small beds of flowers or fruit. Just under the door there was a neat bed of

yellow fruit. Farther out on the front lawn there was a bed of blue fruit. At the bottom of the lawn there was a large squarish bed of pieces of charcoal and small black stones. A few brownish fruits lay here also . . . off to one side there were several big mushrooms in a heap, and near them were ten freshly picked flowers.

Closely associated with, and possibly related to the bower-birds are the birds of paradise. Of their 42 species, 36 are exclusive to New Guinea and its satellite islands, 2 apiece to the Moluccas and the Queensland rain-forest, while 2 inhabit both New Guinea and Queensland. Although some live in lowland forests, 50 per cent live exclusively above 5,000 feet and one species above 10,000 feet. Fruit mainly, large insects, tree-frogs and small arboreal lizards are their food. Although some species with relatively inconspicuous plumage are, like some bower-birds, apparently monogamous with conventional life-histories, the majority are promiscuous and polygynous, displaying their fantastic plumages with the most flamboyant dance movements, and mating with as many females as they can attract. The latter then wander away to nest, lay and rear young without assistance from the males. The males indeed often associate in clans, with each clan preserving its own display and mating territory.

The adult males are not only gorgeously plumaged, but are further embellished by such exotic adornments as, in Gilliard's words, "skirts, whips, capes, lace-like feathers, twisted enamel-like wires, erectile expandable fans, sabre-shaped tails, patches of mirror-like iridescent plumage", or by more conventional or-namentations such as jade and opal-colored mouths, garishly painted areas of bare skin, or leaf-like wattles. Perhaps these male birds of paradise have now reached the stage of over-specialization, for if no adult males are present at the display grounds, the females will mate with sub-adult males, which do not acquire their complex plumes until they are from two to five years old.

As if this ornamentation were not sufficient attraction in itself, it is advertised by the most extraordinary and spectacular dance displays. The males of some species perform their dances in the trees, "charging and then posturing stiffly with their long lace-like cascades of plumage," to quote Gilliard again. "Some hang on shimmering, pendulous mosses beneath [branches] . . . some dance on low vines or on the ground, alternately freezing then spinning with their circular feather-skirting extended ballerina-like." Others, like the blue birds of paradise, which have only been observed in captivity, display while hanging head down from their perches; while two species prepare, like bowerbirds, special display grounds. The magnificent bird of paradise, for example, clears all the litter of leaves and twigs from a 15-foot circle of ground beneath his perching tree, and then spends hours stripping the leaves from any saplings overhanging the arena, thereby permitting vertical shafts of sunlight to illuminate the reds, yellows and greens of his gorgeous plumage and the two long, thin coiled feathers that project from his short tail, as he dances. He passes most of the daylight hours alone at his court, preening on a perch at its edge, though Austin Rand has described how from time to time one male would interrupt his preening routine to fly into his arena and pull off a leaf or two, worry at a twig, or drop to the ground to flick away a bit of debris that had drifted in. Then he might display on one of the saplings before returning to his perch. Although this male uttered his characteristic loud, clear *car-car* every now and again only once did a female—a short-tailed brownish bird about 7 inches long—visit the arena and after some preliminary moving about, with each bird advancing and retreating, hop up to a sapling immediately above the male. This stimulated the male to his full display. Clinging to a vertical sapling, he stretched out his body horizontally, with his green breast-shield flattened and spread and his yellow ruff raised to frame his head, retaining this posture until she hopped down the sapling and mated with him.

The most fantastic plumages and sophisticated displays are exhibited by the seven species of *Paradisea*, the males of some of which display in groups high up the trees, co-ordinating their dance movements and spreading their plumes in unison at the climax of their performance. Thus, although a party or *sacaleli* of only two greater birds of paradise is sufficient to initiate a dance, as many as a dozen or a score of these crow-sized, coffee-brown birds with metallic green and straw-yellow heads, 2-foot long tufts of lacy golden-orange plumes at their flanks and two central elongated tail-wires will dance together in certain selected trees. These trees have immense heads of spreading but rather sparse foliage, and the males display on slightly sloping branches that rise in tiers from 20 to 40 feet above the ground, with the male with the longest plumes usually occupying the middle or main perch. In the intervals of flying excitedly from branch to branch the birds display, and Wallace describes how:

> The wings are raised vertically over the back, the head is bent down and stretched out, and the long plumes are raised up and expanded till they form two magnificent golden fans striped with deep red at the base, and fading off into the pale brown tint of the finely divided and softly waving points. The whole bird is then overshadowed by them, the crouching body, yellow head, and emerald green throat forming but the foundation and setting to the golden glory which waves above.

At the climax of their communal dance, which is most animated and prolonged when females are in the vicinity, and which Gilliard termed the "flower display," the males' heads are below the level of their perches; and he describes how in this deeply bowed posture a displaying bird looks as if it is dying:

The mouth is wide open and its eyes glassy. . . . Its wings and long tail-wires slope downwards and its immense plumes stand up straight like a golden fountain. Thus it stands frozen and the only motion is a bewitching one . . . as the thin filaments wave back and forth in the breeze. Like great exotic flowers, the males remain immobile for minutes on end, while the females promenade around, apparently selecting prospective males.

Selected Bibliography

Adamson, Joy. *Forever Free*. New York: Harcourt, Brace, Jovanovich, 1963; London: Collins & Harvill, 1962.

Akeley, Mary L. J. *Carl Akeley's Africa: The Account of the Akeley-Eastman-Pomeroy African Hall Expedition*. New York: Dodd, Mead; London: Gollancz, 1931.

Banks, E. *A Naturalist in Sarawak*. Kuching: The Kuching Press, 1949.

Banks, Martin. "Red Squirrels in Britain." *Animals* 14 (1972): 400–403.

Bazé, William. *Just Elephants*. Trans. by H. M. Burton. London: Elek Books, 1955.

Beccari, Odoardo. *Wanderings in the Great Forests of Borneo: Travel and Researches of a Naturalist in Sarawak*. London: Archibald Constable, 1904.

Beebe, William. *Tropical Wild Life in British Guiana*. New York: New York Zoological Society, 1917.

Bere, Rennie M. *The African Elephant*. London: Barker, 1966.

Bergamini, David, and the Editors of *Life*. *The Land and Wildlife of Australasia*. New York: Time-Life International (Nederland), 1964.

Bergman, Sten. *Through Primitive New Guinea*. Trans. by Maurice Michael. London: Robert Hale, 1957.

Bigg-Wither, Thomas P. *Pioneering in South Brazil: Three Years of Forest and Prairie Life in the Province of Panama*. London, 1878. Reprint, Westport, Conn.: Greenwood Press, 1968.

Bourlière, François. *The Natural History of Mammals: A Field Outline*. New York: Knopf, 1961; London: Harrap, 1955.

Brown, Leslie. *Africa: A Natural History*. New York: Random House; London: Hamish Hamilton, 1965.

Cahalane, Victor H. *Mammals of North America.* New York: Macmillan, 1947, 1966.

Calaby, J. H. "Observations of the Banded Ant-Eater *Myrocobius f. fasciatus* (Marsupialia) with Particular Reference to Its Food Habits." *Proceedings of the Zoological Society of London* 135 (1960): 183–207.

Carpenter, Clarence Ray. "Behaviour of Red Spider Monkeys in Panama." *Journal of Mammalogy* 16 (1935): 171–80.

————. "A Field Study of the Behaviour and Social Relations of the Gibbon." *Comparative Psychology Monographs* 16 (1940): 1–212.

————. "A Field Study of the Behaviour and Social Relations of the Howling Monkeys." *Comparative Psychology Monographs* 10 (1934): 1–168.

————. "The Howlers of Barro Colorado Island." in *Primate Behaviour: Field Studies of Monkeys and Apes,* ed. by Irvin de Vore. New York: Holt, Rinehart & Winston, 1965.

Carr, Archie, and the Editors of *Life. The Land and Wildlife of Africa.* New York: Time-Life International (Nederland), 1964.

Carrington, Richard. *Elephants: A Short Account of Their Natural History, Evolution and Influence on Mankind.* London: Chatto & Windus, 1958.

Chivers, David. "The Monkeys of Barro Colorado Island." *Animals* 11 (1968): 355–59.

Christy, Cuthbert. *Big Game and Pygmies: Experiences of a Naturalist in Central African Forests in Quest of the Okapi.* London: Macmillan, 1924.

Cloudsley-Thompson, J. L. *The Zoology of Tropical Africa.* New York: Norton; London: Weidenfeld & Nicolson, 1969.

Collins, W. B. *The Perpetual Forest.* London: Staple Press, 1958.

Curry-Lindahl, Kai. *Europe: A Natural History.* New York: Random House; London: Hamish Hamilton, 1964.

Cutright, P. R. *Great Naturalists Explore South America.* New York: Macmillan, 1940.

Darling, Frank Fraser. *Natural History in the Highlands and Islands.* London: Collins, 1947.

Davenport, R. K. "The Orang-Utan in Sabah." *Folia Primatilogica* 4 (1966): 247–63.

Dorst, Jean. *South America and Central America: A Natural History.* New York: Random House; London: Hamish Hamilton, 1967.

Durrell, Gerald. *Catch Me a Colobus.* New York: Viking; London: Collins, 1972.

————. *The Overloaded Ark*. New York: Viking; London: Faber & Faber, 1953.

Eggeling, W. J. "Observations on the Ecology of the Budongo Rain Forest, Uganda." *Journal of Ecology* 34 (1947): 20–87.

Egli, Emil, in Schulthess, E. *The Amazon: A Photographic Survey*. Trans. by H. A. Frey and C. Wayland. New York: Simon & Schuster, 1963. (Published in Great Britain as *The Amazon*. London: Collins, 1962.)

Eibl-Eibesfeldt, Irenaus and Eleonore. "The Workers' Bodyguard." *Animals* 2 (1968): 16–17.

Fisher, James, and Peterson, Roger Tory. *The World of Birds*. London: Macdonald, 1964.

Fossey, Dian. "Making Friends with Mountain Gorillas." *National Geographic Magazine* 137 (1970): 48–67.

————. "More Years with Mountain Gorillas." *National Geographic Magazine* 140 (1971): 574–85.

————. "Vocalisations of the Mountain Gorilla." *Animal Behaviour* 20, 1 (1972): 36–53.

Gandar-Dower, Kenneth C. *The Spotted Lion*. London: Heinemann, 1937.

Gilliard, E. Thomas. *Birds of Paradise and Bower Birds*. New York: Natural History Press; London: Weidenfeld & Nicolson, 1969.

Groves, Colin P. *Gorillas*. New York: Arco; London: Barker, 1970.

Grzimek's Animal Encyclopedia. New York and London: Van Nostrand Reinhold, n.d.

Guenther, Konrad. *A Naturalist in Brazil*. London: Allen & Unwin, 1931.

Hardy, G. A. "Squirrel Cache of Fungi." *Canadian Field Naturalist* 63 (1949): 86–87.

Harrisson, Barbara. "The Man of the Woods at Home." *Animals* 1 (1963): 7–10.

————. *Orang-Utan*. New York: Doubleday, 1963; London: Collins, 1962.

Haviland, Maud D. *Forest, Steppe and Tundra*. New York and Cambridge: Cambridge University Press, 1926.

Hoogerwerf, A. *Udjung Kulon: The Land of the Last Javan Rhinoceros*. Leiden: E. J. Brill, 1970.

Humboldt, Baron A. von. *Personal Narrative of Travels to the Equinoctial Regions of America During 1799–1804*. London, 1853. Reprint (7 vols. in 6). Trans. by Helen M. Williams. New York: AMS Press, n.d.

Imms, A. D. *Insect Natural History*. London: Collins, 1947.

Keast, A.; Crocker, R. L.; and Christian, C. S. *Biogeography and Ecology in Australia*. New York: Humanities Press; Den Haag: W. Junk., 1959.

Keast, Allen. *Australia and the Pacific Islands: A Natural History*. New York: Random House; London, Hamish Hamilton, 1966.

Kortlandt, Adriaan. "Chimpanzees in the Wild." *Scientific American* 206 (1962): 128–38.

Lange, Algot. *In the Amazon Jungle*. New York: Putnam, 1912.

Lawick-Goodall, Jane van. "The Behavior of Free-Living Chimpanzees in the Gombe Stream Reserve." *Animal Behaviour Monographs* 1 (1968): 161–311.

———. *In the Shadow of Man*. London: Collins; Boston: Houghton Mifflin, 1971.

Lawrence, R. D. *The Place in the Forest*. Camden, N.J.: Nelson, 1968; London: Michael Joseph, 1967.

Leopold, A. Starker. *Wildlife of Mexico*. Berkeley: University of California Press, 1959.

Linblad, Jan. *Journey to Red Birds*. Trans. by Gwynne Vevers. New York: Hill & Wang; London: Collins, 1969.

McKie, Ronald. *The Company of Animals*. London and Sydney: Angus & Robertson, 1965; New York: Harcourt, Brace & World, 1966.

Marais, Eugène. *The Soul of the White Ant*. Trans. by Winifred de Kok. London: Jonathan Cape & Anthony Blond, 1971.

Merfield, Fred. *Gorilla Hunter*. New York: Farrar, Straus & Cudahy, 1956. (Published in Great Britain as *Gorillas Were My Neighbours*. London: Longmans, Green, 1956.)

Miller, Leo E. *In the Wilds of South America*. London: T. Fisher Unwin, 1919.

Milne, Lorus J, and Milne, Margery. *The Arena of Life: The Dynamics of Ecology*. London: Allen & Unwin, 1972.

———. *The Senses of Animals and Men*. New York: Atheneum; London: André Deutsch, 1963.

Norris, Ted. "Ceylon Sloth Bear." *Animals* 12 (1969): 300–303.

Owen, Dennis E. *Animal Ecology in Tropical Africa*. San Francisco: W. H. Freeman; London: Oliver & Boyd, 1966.

Perry, Richard. *Bears*. New York: Arco; London: Barker, 1970.

———. *In the High Grampians*. London: Lindsay Drummond, 1948.

———. *Life at the Sea's Frontiers*. New York: Taplinger; Newton Abbot: David & Charles, 1974.

————. *The World of the Jaguar*. New York: Taplinger; Newton Abbot: David & Charles, 1970.

————. *The World of the Tiger*. New York: Atheneum, 1965; London: Cassell, 1964.

Petter, Jean Jacques. "The Lemurs of Madagascar" in *Primate Behaviour: Field Studies of Monkeys and Apes*, ed. by Irvin de Vore. New York: Holt, Rinehart & Winston, 1965.

Pfeffer, Pierre. *Asia: A Natural History*. New York: Random House; London: Hamish Hamilton, 1968.

Pitman, Charles R. S. *The Elephant in Uganda*. London: Rowland Ward, 1953.

————. *A Game Warden Among His Charges*. London: Nisbet, 1931.

Pizzey, Graham. *Animals and Birds in Australia*. Melbourne: Cassell (Australia), 1966.

————. "Lyrebirds of Sherbrooke." *Animals* 2 (1963): 356–57.

Prater, S. H. *The Book of Indian Animals*. Bombay: Bombay Natural History Society, n.d.

Ramsbottom, John. *Mushrooms and Toadstools: A Study of the Activities of Fungi*. New York: Dutton; London: Collins, 1953.

Rand, Austin L. "Birds of Paradise." *Animals* 8 (1966): 346–55.

Ratcliffe, Francis. *Flying Fox and Drifting Sand: The Adventures of a Biologist in Australia*. London: Angus & Robertson, 1948.

————; Gay, F. J.; and Greaves, T. *Australian Termites: The Biology, Recognition and Economic Importance of the Common Species*. Melbourne: Commonwealth Scientific and Industrial Research Organisation, Australia, 1952.

Reader's Digest Association. *The Living World of Animals*. New York and London, 1970.

Reynolds, Vernon. *The Apes: The Gorilla, Chimpanzee, Orangutan and Gibbon—Their History and Their World*. New York: Dutton, 1967; London: Cassell, 1967.

————. *Budongo: A Forest and Its Chimpanzees*. New York: Doubleday; London: Methuen, 1965.

Ripley, S. Dillon. *The Land and Wildlife of Tropical Asia*. New York: Time-Life International, 1964.

Sanderson, Ivan T. *The Dynasty of Abu: A History and Natural History of the Elephants and Their Relatives Past and Present*. New York: Curtis Publishing, 1960.

————. *The Natural Wonders of North America*. London: Hamish Hamilton, 1962.

Schaller, George B. *The Deer and the Tiger: A Study of Wildlife in India*. Chicago: University of Chicago Press, 1967.

———. *The Mountain Gorilla: Ecology and Behaviour*. Chicago: University of Chicago Press, 1963.

———. "The Orangutan in Sarawak." *Zoologica* 46 (1961): 73–82.

———. *The Year of the Gorilla*. Chicago: University of Chicago Press, 1964; London: Collins, 1965.

Scheithauer, Walter. *Hummingbirds: Flying Jewels*. Trans. by Gwynne Vevers. London: Barker, 1967.

Schneirla, T. C. *Army Ants: A Study in Social Organisation*. San Francisco: W. H. Freeman, 1971.

Schulthess, E. *The Amazon: A Photographic Survey*. Trans. by H. A. Frey and C. Wayland. New York: Simon & Schuster, 1963. (Published in Great Britain as *The Amazon*. London: Collins, 1962.)

Schumacher, Eugen. *The Last of the Wild: On the Track of Rare Animals*. Trans. by Gwynne Vevers and Winwood Read. London: Collins, 1968.

Schurz, William Lytle. *Brazil: The Infinite Country*. New York: Dutton, 1961; London: Robert Hale, 1962.

Selenka, Emil, in *Grzimek's Animal Encyclopedia*. New York and London: Van Nostrand Reinhold, n.d.

Seshadri, Balakrishna. *The Twilight of India's Wildlife*. New York: Fernhill House; London: John Baker, 1969.

Sharland, Michael. *A Territory of Birds*. London: Angus & Robertson, 1964.

Shaw, William T. "Moisture and Its Relation to the Cone-Storing Habit of the Western Pine Squirrel." *Journal of Mammalogy* 17 (1936): 337–49.

Shorten, Monica. *Squirrels*. London: Collins, 1954.

Sielmann, Heinz. *My Year with the Woodpeckers*. Trans. by Sidney Lighterman. London: Barrie & Rockcliffe, 1959.

Sikes, Sylvia. *The Natural History of the African Elephant*. New York: American Elsevier; London: Weidenfeld & Nicolson, 1971.

Skaife, S. H. *Dwellers in Darkness: An Introduction to the Study of Termites*. London: Longmans, Green, 1955.

Smith, Anthony. *Mato Grosso: Last Virgin Land*. London: Michael Joseph; New York: E. P. Dutton, 1971.

Sparks, John, and Soper, Tony. *Owls: Their Natural and Unnatural History*. New York: Taplinger; Newton Abbot: David & Charles, 1970.

Stracey, P. D. *Tigers*. London: Barker, 1966.

Sudd, John. *An Introduction to the Behaviour of Ants.* New York: St. Martin's Press; London: Edward Arnold, 1967.

Troughton, Ellis. *Furred Animals of Australia.* Sydney: Angus & Robertson, 1965.

Turnbull-Kemp, Peter. *The Leopard.* San Francisco: Tri-Ocean, 1968; Cape Town: Howard Timmins, 1967.

Up de Graff, F. W. *Head-Hunters of the Amazon.* New York, 1927.

Wallace, Alfred Russell. *The Malay Archipelago.* London: Macmillan 1869. Reprint. Gloucester, Mass.: Peter Smith, n.d.

Warham, John. "Birds That Build Bowers." *Animals* 2 (1963): 286–89.

Zahl, Paul A. *The Lost World.* New York: Knopf, 1939.

Index